Secretary's Book
of
INSTANT LETTERS

Jean C. Vermes

PARKER PUBLISHING COMPANY, INC.

West Nyack, N.Y.

HOW TO USE THIS BOOK

This instant letter writer is planned to save the secretary hours of time spent in composing letters for herself or her employer. Ordinary form letters can only act as a guide, and rewriting them is sometimes harder than creating your own.

The letters in this book can be adapted to fit nearly every need, through a multiple choice of words, phrases, and paragraphs. Suppose, for example, your executive asks you to write a letter over his signature, adjusting a certain complaint. You would look either under the heading, *Complaints, Adjusting* or *Adjustment of Complaints,* find the type of letter you want, and copy it. In the letter there will be spaces to allow for your own names and dates. There will also be alternate words for your selection, as well as alternate paragraphs from which you can choose.

The book is divided, for your convenience, into three sections, alphabetized under subject for easy reference. Part I is separated into three chapters, supplying letters written over your own signature either routinely, optionally, or in your employer's absence. Part II is composed of letters to be written by you for your employer's signature, although they can always be adapted for your own. Part III gives you directions for setting up a file of individual instant letters, suited to those specialized needs which cannot be covered in a general way. It concludes with information on letter styles and forms of address.

With this book as a reference, you will be able to take care of ordinary correspondence for yourself and your employer with speed, efficiency, and a minimum of effort. For instance:

Sample #1

Here is a sample of a complete form letter to suit a situation such as cancelling appointments for your employer in his absence. This letter contains an italicized key paragraph, and it is followed by two alternate paragraphs, to be used as the occasion requires. The introductory paragraph remains the same throughout. Under *Letters Written in Employer's Absence,* in Part I of the book, you will find the listing, *Appointments, Cancelling.* The letter follows:

APPOINTMENTS, CANCELLING

a. Breaking Suggested Date

Dear _____:

(executive's name) is away from the office and is not expected back until (date).

I have checked (name) schedule and find that (s)he has other plans for the date you suggest. However, I shall call your letter to (name) attention as soon as (s)he returns and perhaps you can make other arrangements.

Cordially,

b. Changing Date Scheduled

I regret that (name) will not be able to keep your appointment on (date) as scheduled. Let me know if you would like to arrange for another meeting at a later date.

c. Postponing Meeting Until Later Time

However, before (name) left (s)he indicated that it would be more convenient to meet with you at some later time. Will you be good enough to get in touch with us in a few days/weeks/months?

Suggested Use

If your employer, Mr. Adams, won't return in time to keep an appointment with a Mr. Bates who expected to see him, you would choose paragraph *B* or *Changing Date Scheduled.* The result would be a letter like this:

Dear Mr. Bates:

    Mr. Adams is away from the office and is not
expected back until May 15th.
    I regret that Mr. Adams will not be able to
keep his appointment with you on the 14th as scheduled. Let me know if you would like to arrange for
another meeting at a later date.

Cordially,

Sample #2

    Another typical form letter is this one for your employer's signature,
following a sales call made in person or by telephone. You would find it listed
under *Sales, Sales Promotion,* and also cross referenced under the *Follow-Up*
listing, both in Part II, *Letters Usually Signed by Employer.* This letter
contains a number of italicized words at key points, from which you can
choose those that fit your requirements. For example:

SALES, SALES PROMOTION

(6) Following a Call

Dear _____:

    Last (date) I spoke to you about our new <u>pro-
posal/product(s)/shipment/service/design,</u> telling
you of the prices now available. Since you were not
then in a position to make a decision, we agreed
that I contact you at a more convenient time.
    Now (customer's name), we are well into
<u>spring/summer/fall/winter.</u> I'm still confident that
the suggested <u>proposal/product(s)/shipment/service/
design</u> can <u>save/make</u> you money, so I'd advise you
to consider placing your order in the next <u>day/week/
month</u> or two.
    If you have any further questions I'll be
happy to answer them.

Cordially,

Suggested Use

    Following is a sample use of this instant letter by a secretary whose
employer has paid a sales call on a Mr. Crandell about a new product, which
he wishes followed up with a reminder that time is passing by if the customer
wants to save money.

Dear Mr. Crandell:

     Last October I spoke to you about our new product, telling you of the prices now available. Since you were not then in a position to make a decision, we agreed that I contact you at a more convenient time.

     Now, Mr. Crandell, we are well into winter. I'm still confident that the suggested product can save you money, so I'd advise you to consider placing your order in the next week or two.

     If you have any further questions I'll be happy to answer them.

Cordially,

     Secretaries who make the effort to write their own letters are liberating themselves from humdrum routine in an ideal way. After a modest start, they can go on to a wider and wider takeover of the correspondence and other business details. As they gradually ease themselves into positions of importance, the career potentials are unlimited.

JEAN C. VERMES

CONTENTS

PART II

LETTERS USUALLY SIGNED BY EMPLOYER

PART III

APPENDIX

PART ONE

Letters Usually Signed by Secretary

Chapter 1 LETTERS ROUTINELY HANDLED BY SECRETARY

Contents

ADJUSTMENTS IN ACCOUNTS

(1) Bank Account Errors

Gentlemen.

Today we received the (employer's name) check-ing account monthly statement covering deposits and withdrawals from (date) to (date).

There is some discrepancy between your figures and our own, which we would appreciate your recheck-ing. You show a deposit/withdrawal of (amount), which does not appear on our records.

We do, however, have a deposit slip/cancelled check for (amount), which is not accounted for in your statement.

We show a bank balance for (employer's name) of (amount), and would like verification of our figures.

Sincerely,

(2) Charge Account, Office Supply

Gentlemen:

Today we received (employer's name) monthly statement for (amount) covering office supplies for the month of (date).

There is some discrepancy between your figures and our own, and we would appreciate your recheck-ing. You show a purchase of (supply) on (date) for (amount), which does not appear on our records.

Enclosed is our check for this month's state-ment in the corrected amount of (amount). Please credit (employer's name) in full.

Sincerely,

(3) Travel Card Account—Cancellations Not Credited

Gentlemen:

Your statement of (date) for the (employer's name) account (number) includes a charge for (amount) for a (date) flight from (place) to (place). We purchased these tickets on (date). However, we cancelled the flight by telephone on (date), and returned the tickets to you at that time.

Enclosed is (employer's name) check for the amount of your (date) statement, minus the charge for the flight. Please credit (employer's name) account in full.

Sincerely,

(4) Travel Card Account—Incorrect Amounts

Gentlemen:

Your statement of (date) charges the (employer's name) account (amount) for <u>meals</u>/<u>room</u>/<u>telephone calls</u>/<u>merchandise</u> <u>at</u>/<u>from</u> the (name) <u>hotel</u>/<u>motel</u>/<u>restaurant</u>/<u>store</u> in (place) on (date.) According to the record of charge, the total should be (amount), instead of the amount on the statement.

Enclosed is (employer's name) check for this month's statement in the corrected amount. Please credit (employer's name) account (number) in full.

Very truly yours,

INFORMATION, SECURING
(1) Hotel Rooms, Availability and Rates

Gentlemen:

Will you please send me by return mail the rates for <u>a single room</u>/<u>a double room</u>/<u>a suite</u>/<u>single rooms</u>/<u>double rooms</u>/<u>suites</u> to accommodate (number) of our <u>executives</u>/<u>salesmen</u>/<u>representatives</u>/<u>employees</u> from (day, date) through (day, date).

I would appreciate your prompt reply, since I must complete reservations as soon as possible.

Cordially,

(2) Plane Schedules

Gentlemen:

Will you please help me route my employer, (name), from (place) by (airline) to (place), via the following cities, with stopovers as indicated:

(city)   (length of stopover)
(city)   (length of stopover)
(city)   (length of stopover)

(Name) expects to leave (place) on the morning/afternoon/evening of (date) and must be in (place) at (time) of (date). (S)He wants to remain in (final destination) through (date), and then wishes a direct flight back to (place) if possible.

Thank you for your prompt attention.

Cordially,

(3) Restaurant Facilities

Gentlemen:

Our (name of person or department) wishes to entertain at breakfast/luncheon/dinner at (name of restaurant) on (date) at (time).

This will be a party for (number) people, and a private dining room would be preferable/is not essential. We will/will not need the services of a wine steward/bartender, and we will choose our menu in advance/food from your regular menu.

Please let us have information as to the accommodations available, and the approximate cost, including gratuities, and tax, (and number and kind of drinks, if any), by return mail if possible.

Cordially,

(4) Theater Tickets

Gentlemen:

   Do you have (number) <u>orchestra/mezzanine/box</u>
seats available for the <u>afternoon/evening</u> of (date)
for (name of play, concert, sports event, etc.)?
(Number) of our <u>executives/salesmen/employees/</u>
<u>clients/customers</u> will be in (city) at that time,
and we would like to obtain good seats for them.

   If you can accommodate us, please let us know
the price of the tickets so we may send you a check
without delay.

Cordially,

ORDERS, PLACING

(1) Office Equipment

Dear _____:

   I should like to place an order, to be billed to
(name of company) for the following:

   (number)   (brand name)   <u>typewriter(s)/</u>
Size: <u>file(s)/adding</u>
Color: <u>machine(s)/lamp(s)/</u>
Description: <u>desk(s)/chair(s)/</u>
Identification Number (if any): <u>other</u>

   Will you please make delivery as soon as possible to the above address, room (number), attention
of the undersigned.

Sincerely,

(2) Office Supplies

Dear _____:

   Please send the following as soon as you can,
and <u>bill to our account/send us a bill</u>:

   (amount)   (brand name)   <u>bond paper/second</u>
                                <u>sheets/carbon</u>
                                <u>paper/typewriter</u>

<u>ribbons/manila</u> <u>envelopes/white</u> <u>envelopes/scratch</u> <u>pads/pencils/ball-</u> <u>point pens/steno</u> <u>pads/erasers/sta-</u> <u>tionery/other</u>

Size:

Description:

Kindly deliver to the above address, room (number) attention of the undersigned.

Sincerely,

RESERVATIONS, CANCELLING, CHANGING

(1) Hotel Rooms

a. Cancelling

Gentlemen:

Several <u>weeks</u>/<u>days</u> ago, I reserved (number) room(s) for out (title(s), (name(s), for the night(s) of (date, dates).

<u>He/She/They will not be able to make the trip</u> <u>to (place) at this time. Will you please send me a</u> <u>written acknowledgment of this cancellation</u>?

Cordially,

b. Changing

<u>He/She/They will not be able to make the trip</u> <u>to (place) on that date; but instead will be there</u> <u>on (date, dates). Will you please send me a written</u> <u>confirmation of this change</u>?

(2) Plane Flights

a. Cancelling

Gentlemen:

On (date) I reserved (number) <u>first class/</u> <u>tourist class</u> seat(s) for my employer(s) on your

flight (number) from (place) to (place), leaving at
(time) on (day of the week) (date) with return to
(place) scheduled for (date).

He/She/They will not be able to make the trip
to (place) at this time. Will you please send me an
acknowledgment of this cancellation and refund our
money/credit our account?

Cordially,

b. Changing

He/She/They will not be able to make the trip
to (place) at that time, but instead will go there
on (date), and return on (date). Please send me confirmation of this change in flight schedule.

(3) Restaurant Facilities

a. Cancelling Reservations (no refund)

Gentlemen:

On (date) I reserved (number) tables for (number) people for breakfast/luncheon/dinner at (time)
on (date) for our (name) in the (name) room.
There has been a change in plans and the occasion will have to be postponed. Will you, therefore,
be good enough to cancel the reservation?
Thank you very much.

Cordially,

b. Cancelling Reservations (refund)

There has been a change in plans and the occasion will have to be postponed. Will you be good
enough, therefore, to cancel the reservation and return our check for (amount)?

c. Changing Reservation (date)

There has been a change in plans and the occasion will have to be postponed until (date) at (time). Will you be good enough to make the same arrangements for that date and send us a written confirmation?

(4) Theater Tickets

a. Cancelling Reservations (refund)

Gentlemen:

On (date) I purchased (number) orchestra/mezzanine/box seats for the afternoon/evening of (date) for (name of play, concert, sports event, etc.).

There has been a change in plans and we will be unable to use the enclosed tickets. We would appreciate your refunding their price, making check payable to (name).

Thank you very much.

Sincerely,

b. Changing Reservation (ticket exchange)

As there has been a change in plans, we will be unable to use the enclosed tickets. We would appreciate your exchanging them for similar seats on (date) or (date).

RESERVATIONS, CONFIRMING VERBAL

(1) Hotel Rooms

Gentlemen:

This will confirm reservation made by phone on (date) for a single room/a double room/a suite/ single rooms/ double rooms/suites to accommodate (number) of our executives/salesmen/employees from (day, date) through (day, date), at a daily rate of (amount, <u>European</u>/<u>American</u>/<u>Modified American</u> plan.

Sincerely,

(2) Plane Flights

    a. Charge Account

Gentlemen:

    This will confirm reservation made by phone on (date) for (employer's name) for (number) <u>first/tourist</u> class seat(s) on your flight (number) from (place) to (place) for (time) on (day, date), returning on flight (number) from (place) to (place) at (time) on (day, date).

    <u>Kindly charge to (name of account) (credit card name) account (number), and forward tickets by return mail</u>.

    Thank you very much.

Sincerely,

    b. Check Payment in Advance

    <u>Our check for (amount) is enclosed. Kindly forward tickets by return mail</u>.

    c. Check Payment on Receipt

    <u>Our check for (amount) will be forwarded to you as soon as the tickets are received</u>.

(3) Restaurant Facilities

    a. Advance Payment

Gentlemen:

    This will confirm telephone reservation made on (date) for (number) tables for (number) people for <u>breakfast</u>/<u>luncheon</u>/<u>dinner</u> at (time) on (date) for our (name), in the (name) room.

    <u>Enclosed is our check for (amount) to cover the</u>

cost of food, gratuities, and tax for (number), exclusive of/including (number and type of) drinks.

b. Charge Account

The cost of food, gratuities, and tax, includ-
ing/excluding drinks, for this occasion will be
charged to (name of account) (credit card name), account (number).

(4) Theater Tickets

a. By Mail

Gentlemen:

This will confirm reservation made by phone on
(date) for (number) orchestra/mezzanine/box seats
for the afternoon/evening of (date) for (name of
play, concert, sports event, etc.).
Our check for (amount) is enclosed. Kindly forward tickets in the attached stamped, self-addressed
envelope.

b. By Messenger

Our check for (amount) is enclosed. Kindly give
tickets to messenger.

c. Pick-up at Box Office

Our check for (amount) is enclosed. Kindly hold
the tickets in the name of (name) for pick-up at the
box office on (date).

RESERVATIONS, MAKING BY MAIL

(1) Hotel Rooms

Gentlemen:

I should like to make a reservation for (number) single room(s)/double room(s)/suite(s) to ac-

commodate (number) of our <u>executives</u>/<u>salesmen</u>/<u>em-</u>
<u>ployees</u> from (day, date) through (day, date), <u>Euro-</u>
<u>pean</u>/<u>American</u>/<u>Modified American</u> plan.

    <u>He</u>/<u>She</u>/<u>They</u> will arrive around (time of day),
and will pick up the reservation in the name of (employer's name).

Cordially,

(2) Plane Flights

a. Check Payment

Gentlemen:

    I should like to make a reservation for (em-
ployer's name) for (number) <u>first</u>/<u>tourist</u> class
seat(s) on your flight (number) from (place) to
(place) for (time) on (day, date), returning from
(place) to (place) at (time) on (day, date).
    <u>Check for (amount) is enclosed. Kindly forward</u>
<u>tickets by return mail</u>.

Sincerely,

b. Charge Account

    <u>Kindly charge to (name of account) (credit card</u>
<u>name) account (number), and forward tickets by re-</u>
<u>turn mail</u>.

(3) Restaurant Facilities

a. Check Payment

Gentlemen:

    Will you please reserve (number) tables for
(number) people for <u>breakfast</u>/<u>luncheon</u>/<u>dinner</u> at
(time) on (date) for (employer's name), in the
(name) room. We <u>will</u>/<u>will not</u> desire <u>wine</u>/<u>cocktails</u>
<u>and</u>/<u>or</u> the services of a <u>wine steward</u>/<u>bartender</u>.
We would like to <u>plan our menu in advance</u>/<u>choose our</u>
<u>food from your regular menu</u>.

Check will follow after we receive an estimate
of the cost of food, gratuities, and tax, exclusive
of/including (number and type of)/drinks.

b. Charge Account

The cost of food, gratuities, and tax for (number), including/exclusive of drinks, is to be
charged to (name of account) (credit card name), account (number).

(4) Theater Tickets

Gentlemen:

Enclosed is our check for (amount) for (number)
orchestra/mezzanine/box seats for the afternoon/
evening of (date) for (name of play, concert, sports
event, etc.). Our second choice of date would be
(date).

A stamped, self-addressed return envelope is
enclosed for your convenience.

Sincerely,

Chapter 2 LETTERS WRITTEN IN EMPLOYER'S ABSENCE

Contents

ACKNOWLEDGMENTS WITHOUT ANSWERS

(1) General Acknowledgments

Dear _____:

Because (executive's name) is out of town until
(date), I'm acknowledging your letter of (date).
(S)He will give it immediate attention upon his/her
return and you may expect to hear from us shortly
thereafter.

Sincerely,

(2) Information Received

a. Will Call to Executive's Attention

Dear _____:

(Executive's name) is away from the office and
is not expected back until (date).
The information concerning (subject) will be
called to (name) attention as soon as (s)he returns.
Thank you so much for sending it to us.

Cordially,

b. Will Pass Along

The information concerning (subject) will be
passed along to (name of person(s), department(s),
and I will call it to (name) attention as soon as
(s)he returns.

(3) Letters Received

a. Will Call to Executive's Attention

Dear _____ :

(Executive's name) is away from the office and is not expected back until (date).

<u>Your letter concerning (subject) will be called to (name) attention as soon as (s)he returns, and you will hear from us further at that time.</u>

Sincerely,

b. Will Pass Along

<u>A copy of your letter concerning (subject) will be passed along to (name of person(s), department(s), and I will keep the original for (name) to read when (s)he returns.</u>

(4) Material Received

Dear _____ :

This will acknowledge receipt today of (material) which you were good enough to send to (executives's name). (S)He has been looking forward to receiving it and I wanted to let you know the (material) arrived.

(Name) is away from the office and is not expected back until (date). At that time I'm sure (s)he will be in touch with you personally.

Cordially,

(5) Orders Received or Changed

Dear _____ :

This will acknowledge receipt of your <u>order/ change in order</u> for (number) (description) (model number) (merchandise).

(Executive's name) is away from the office and is not expected back until (date). Your request will

be called to <u>his</u>/<u>her</u> attention as soon as (s)he returns. Meantime, I have forwarded your <u>order</u>/<u>change
in order</u> to the <u>factory</u>/<u>warehouse</u>/<u>store</u>/<u>(name of)
department</u>.

Cordially,

(6) Request for Information

    a. Will Call to Executive's Attention

Dear _____:

    This will acknowledge receipt of your letter of
(date), addressed to (executive's name), in connection with (subject).
    <u>(Name) is out of town until (date), but I want
to assure you that your request for information will
be given immediate attention when (s)he returns.</u>

Cordially,

    b. Will Pass Along for Immediate Attention

    <u>(Executive's name) is out of town until (date),
but I want to assure you that your request for information will be given immediate attention, and you
will hear from us shortly.</u>

APOLOGIES FOR DELAY

(1) Acknowledgment of Invitations

    a. When Executive Will Return in Time

Dear _____:

    (Executive's name) is away from the office and
is not expected back until (date).
    <u>I have checked our calendar and (s)he seems to
have (no) other plans for the date you mention, but
this will have to be confirmed. I regret that (s)he
is not here to thank you promptly for your kind invitation. Please accept my apologies for the delay.</u>

b. When Executive Will Not Return in Time

Unfortunately, this will make it impossible for (name) to accept your kind invitation for (date). I regret that (s)he is not able to thank you personally today. Please accept my apologies.

(2) Executive's Delayed Reply

Dear _____:

Because (executive's name) is out of town until (date), I'm acknowledging your letter of (date) concerning (subject). I will bring it to (name) attention as soon as (s)he returns, and you should be hearing from us then.

Please accept my apologies for this unavoidable delay.

Sincerely,

(3) Delay in Filling Order

a. Merchandise

Dear _____:

This will acknowledge receipt of your order for (number) (description) (model number) (merchandise).

(Name) is away from the office and is not expected back until (date). Your order will be processed as soon as (s)he returns.

Please accept my apologies for the delay.

Cordially,

b. Service

This will acknowledge receipt of your order for (type of service).

(4) Delay in Making Purchases

Dear _____:

    Because (executive's name) is out of town until (date), I have had to delay making our purchase of name of equipment/material/service/supply for authorization. I will see that this receives (name) immediate attention upon his/her return, and you will be hearing from us then.

Sincerely,

APPOINTMENTS, CANCELLING & SETTING UP

(1) Cancelling Appointments

    a. Breaking Suggested Date

Dear _____:

    (Executive's name) is away from the office and is not expected back until (date).
    I have checked (name) schedule and find that (s)he has other plans for the date you suggest. However, I shall call your letter to his/her attention as soon as (s)he returns and perhaps you can make other arrangements.

    b. Changing Date Scheduled

    I regret that (executive's name) will not be able to keep your appointment on (date) as scheduled. Let me know if you would like to arrange for another meeting at a later date.

    c. Postponing Meeting with Someone

    Before (s)he left (s)he indicated that it would be more convenient to meet with you at some later time. Will you be good enough to get in touch with us in a few days/weeks/months?

(2) Setting Up Appointments

a. Confirming Previous Date

Dear _____:

    (Executive's name) is away from the office and is not expected back until (date).
    <u>However, before (s)he left, (name) indicated that (s)he would return in plenty of time to keep the appointment with you on (date) at (time), and is looking forward to seeing you.</u>

b. Setting Up for Future Time

    <u>However, I have set up a date for you and (name) on (date) at (time) at (place). Let me know if this is convenient.</u>

c. Setting Up, Time Open

    <u>However, before (s)he left (name) indicated (s)he would like to get together with you upon his/her return. If you will telephone me here I will be happy to set up a date for you to meet.</u>

INFORMATION, SUPPLYING

(1) About Company Literature

Dear _____:

    In (executive's name) absence, I am replying to your inquiry by sending you the enclosed literature which should provide the information you need.
    If there are any further questions, don't hesitate to write again after the (date), when (name) will be able to respond personally.

Sincerely,

(2) About Company Procedures

Dear _____:

    In (executive's name) absence, I am replying to your request for information about our company's (type) procedures.

    Our (type of procedure) operates as follows: (description of operation).

    If there are any further questions, don't hesitate to write again after the (date), when (name) will be happy to assist you.

Cordially,

(3) About Company Products, Services

Dear _____:

    In (executive's name) absence, I am replying to your request for information about our company's products/<u>services</u>.

    Our (name of product(s) or service) <u>is</u>/<u>are</u> available (when) at (price). <u>They</u>/<u>it</u> includes(s) (description of product(s) or service).

    If there are any further questions, don't hesitate to write again after the (date), when (name) will be happy to assist you.

Sincerely,

(4) Concerning Executive's Plans

Dear _____:

    (Executive's name) is away from the office and is not expected back until (date). (S)He is traveling to (place or places) and will be in (place) on (date) at <u>hotel</u>/<u>motel</u>/<u>office</u> where (s)he can be reached at (phone number) or (address), from (date) to (date).

    If I can be of any further assistance, please let me know.

Sincerely,

(5) Reminder of Payments Due

Dear _____:

    In (executive's name) absence, I should like to remind you that you owe us a payment of (amount) on the (product or service) <u>delivered</u>/<u>performed</u> on (date).

    (Name) will return to the office on (date), and I trust that your check will be here by that time.

Sincerely,

INQUIRIES, ANSWERING

(1) About Delivery Dates

Dear _____:

    (Executive's name) is away from the office and is not expected back until (date).

    Meantime, I want to assure you that your order of (date) for (number or quantity) (description of merchandise) will be shipped <u>on</u>/<u>on or about</u> (date).

    Your patronage is appreciated, and we look forward to the opportunity of serving you again.

Sincerely,

(2) About Orders in Works

Dear _____:

    (Executive's name) is away from the office and is not expected back until (date).

    Meantime, I want to assure you that your order of (date) for (number or quantity) (description of merchandise) is being taken care of, and will be shipped to you at the earliest possible date.

    Your patronage is appreciated, and we are more than happy to be of service.

Sincerely,

(3) About Prices

Dear _____ :

    (Executive's name) is away from the office and is not expected back until (date).

    In <u>his</u>/<u>her</u> absence, I am replying to your request for information as to prices with the following list:

(description of product   (number, quantity,   (cost)
        of service)   amount)

(description of product   (number, quantity,   (cost)
        of service)   amount)

    For further details, please get in touch with us again after (date) when (name) will be happy to be of further assistance.

Sincerely,

Chapter 3   LETTERS WRITTEN FOR SECRETARY'S OR EMPLOYER'S SIGNATURE

Contents

Invitations, Declining

Banquets, Conventions (Part II)
Dinner
Luncheon
Meeting
Party
Reception
Speechmaking

Invitations, Extending

Banquets, Conventions (Part II)
Dinner
Luncheon
Meeting
Party
Reception
Speechmaking

Orders, Confirming

Placement of Employer's
Receipt of Another's

ACKNOWLEDGMENTS WHERE NO ANSWER IS REQUIRED
(1) Information Received

Gentlemen:

Thank you so much for sending the information requested regarding (subject).

This will be very helpful, and we/I appreciate your taking the trouble to assist us/me.

If we/I can ever reciprocate in any way please let us/me know.

Cordially,

(2) Letter Received

Dear _____:

Thank you so much for your letter of (date), concerning (subject).

We/I appreciate your taking the trouble to write us/me concerning this matter, and we/I will give it serious consideration.

Always happy to hear from you.

Sincerely,

(3) Material Received

Dear _____:

Thank you so much for the (material) which arrived today/yesterday/the other day.

We/I can make good use of it, and we/I appreciate your sending it along.

It was nice of you to go to all that trouble.

Sincerely,

(4) Order Received

Dear _____:

This will acknowledge receipt of your order for
(number) (description) (model number) (merchandise).

Thank you very much for deciding/continuing to
do business with us. It is very gratifying.

Your order will be processed and shipped just
as soon as possible, and we look forward to serving
you again very soon.

Cordially,

APPOINTMENTS, REFUSING

(1) For the Present

Dear _____:

Thank you for your letter of (date), suggesting
that we/you and (name) get together on (date) to
discuss (subject).

Unfortunately, due to an unusually full schedule, I/(s)he won't be able to keep any additional
appointments at that time.

Will you be good enough to get in touch in a
few days/weeks/months, when we/I will be happy to
arrange for a meeting?

Cordially,

(2) Indefinitely

Dear _____:

Thank you for your letter of (date), suggesting

that we/you and (name) get together on (date) to
discuss (subject).

Right now I/we do not feel that such a meeting
would accomplish any worthwhile results, and I/we
would rather postpone it until a later date.

I/We appreciate your interest, and will be in
touch with you when we feel the time is more pro-
pitious.

Sincerely,

APPOINTMENTS, SETTING UP

(1) Employer Wants to Call

    a. Fixing Time

Dear _____:

There are details I/(or executive's name) would
like very much to discuss with you in connection
with (subject).

How would you like to have me/him/her drop by
on (date) at (time)? I/(s)he would enjoy seeing you
and getting your reactions. If this is not convenient, let me/us know what time you would prefer.

Cordially,

    b. Leaving Time Open

How about a meeting some time in the near future? I/(s)he would enjoy seeing you and getting
your reactions. Let me/us know what time would be
convenient for me/(or executive's name) to call on
you, and I/we will consider it a definite date.

(2) Employer Wants Someone to Call

    a. Fixing Time

Dear _____:

There are details I/(or executive's name) would
like very much to discuss with you in connection
with (subject).

How about dropping by on (date) at (time)? I/ (s)he would enjoy seeing you and getting your re- actions. If this is not convenient, let me/us know what time you would prefer.

I/we will be waiting to hear from you.

Cordially,

b. Leaving Time Open

How about a meeting some time in the near fu- ture? I/(s)he would enjoy seeing you and getting your reactions. Let me/us know what time would be convenient for you to drop by, and I/we will con- sider it a definite date.

(3) Someone Wants to Call on Employer

a. Asking Them to Phone

Dear _____ :

It is good to hear from you, and I/(or execu- tive's name) would like to talk about (subject) with you.

Please call me/my secretary at (number) and let me/her know when it will be convenient for us/you to meet.

I/we look forward to seeing you.

Cordially,

b. Confirming Time

It will be convenient for me/him/her to see you at the time you suggest: (day) at (hour).

c. Setting Time

The most convenient time for me/him/her to see you would be (day) at (hour). I/we hope this fits in with your plans.

INFORMATION, SECURING

(1) About Someone's Products

Dear _____:

    We are interested in the purchase of <u>a</u>/<u>some</u>
(name and description of products), and would appreciate any information you can send us regarding
yours.

    We would like to have details concerning <u>size</u>/
<u>models</u>/<u>weight</u>/<u>colors</u>/<u>materials</u>/<u>finish</u>/<u>prices</u> and
availability at present. We would also like our name
put on your mailing list for the future.

    May we hear from you soon?

Sincerely,

(2) About Someone's Services

Dear _____:

    We are interested in using a (description) ser-
vice, and would like any information you can send us
regarding yours.

    We would appreciate some details as to rates,
and the amount of <u>time</u>/<u>labor</u>/<u>work</u> covered by each
price.

    It would also be helpful if we could know the
earliest possible date that your service would be
available to us.

Sincerely,

(3) About Someone's Statistics

Dear _____:

    In connection with <u>a study</u>/<u>a survey</u>/<u>some re-
search</u> <u>I am</u>/<u>we are</u> conducting, <u>I</u>/<u>we</u> need some sta-
tistics on (subject).

    If you have any information you think would be
helpful, <u>I</u>/<u>we</u> would appreciate your sending it

along. I/we will, of course, give your organization full credit for your assistance.

May I/we hear from you soon?

Cordially,

INFORMATION, SUPPLYING

(1) About Company Literature

Dear _____:

Thank you for your interest in our company. We are enclosing/sending you separately some descriptive literature which will give you details of our operation.

If there is any further information which we can supply, please feel free to write us again.

Cordially,

(2) About Company Procedures

Dear _____:

We appreciate your interest in our (kind of) operations, and we will be glad to describe them for you. In this connection, it is customary for us to proceed as follows:

(Explanation)

If there is any further information which we can supply, please feel free to write us again.

Cordially,

(3) About Company Products

Dear _____:

We appreciate your interest in our products. The (name and description of product or products) comes/come in size/color/material/design, and is/are available at the following prices:

(product)	(price) per (quantity)/each
(product)	(price) per (quantity)/each
(product)	(price) per (quantity)/each

If there is any further information we can supply, please feel free to write us again.

Cordially,

(4) About Company Services

Dear _____:

We appreciate your interest in our services. Our (description) service is available hourly/daily/weekly/monthly/yearly/(X) times a year, and costs (price) per hour/day/week/month/year.

For this charge, you are entitled to (description in detail).

If there is any further information we can supply, please feel free to write us again. We hope to be able to serve you in the near future.

Cordially,

INQUIRIES, ANSWERING

(1) About Delivery Dates

Dear _____:

In reply to your inquiry, I/we want to assure you that your order of (date) for (number or quantity) of (description of merchandise) will be shipped on/on or about (date).

Your patronage is appreciated, and I/we look forward to the opportunity of serving you again.

Sincerely,

(2) About Orders in Works

Dear _____:

In reply to your inquiry, I/we want to assure you that your order of (date) for (number or quanti-

ty) of (description of merchandise) is being processed, and will be shipped to you <u>on (date)</u>/<u>at the
earliest possible date</u>.

Your patronage is appreciated and <u>I</u>/<u>we</u> <u>am</u>/<u>are</u>
more than happy to be of service.

Cordially,

(3) About Prices of Products or Service

    a. Product

Dear _____:

In reply to your request for prices of our (description of product or service), the following
will give you some idea of their range:
<u>(description of product)</u> <u>(cost)</u> <u>(number or quantity)</u>
<u>(description of product)</u> <u>(cost)</u> <u>(number or quantity)</u>
If there is any further information we can sup-
ply, please feel free to write us again. We hope to
be able to serve you in the near future.

Cordially,

    b. Service

<u>(description of service)</u>	<u>(cost)</u>	per hour/<u>day</u>/ <u>week</u>/<u>month</u>/ <u>year</u>
<u>(description of service)</u>	<u>(cost)</u>	per hour/<u>day</u>/ <u>week</u>/<u>month</u>/ <u>year</u>

INVITATIONS, ACCEPTING

(1) Dinner

Dear _____:

Thank you for your dinner invitation for (day
of week) the (date). <u>I</u>/<u>(employer's name)</u> <u>am</u>/<u>is</u> free
that evening, and will be glad to meet and talk with
you about (subject).

I/(s)he will be at the (place) at (time) sharp, and look(s) forward to seeing you.

Cordially,

(2) Luncheon

Dear _____:

Thank you for your luncheon invitation for (day of week) the (date). I/(employer's name) am/is free for lunch on that day, and will be glad to meet and talk with you about (subject).

I/(s)he will be at the (place) at (time) sharp, and look(s) forward to seeing you.

Cordially,

(3) Meeting, Party, Reception

Dear _____:

Thank you very much for your invitation to join the (name of organization) at the (place) on (date). I/(name of employer) shall/will be happy to be there at (time) to take part in the meeting/festivities/reception, and look(s) forward to it with pleasure.

Cordially,

(4) Speechmaking

   a. Accepting Topic

Dear _____:

I/(employer's name) shall/will be very happy to accept your kind invitation to speak at the breakfast/dinner/luncheon/meeting you are having on (day, date) for (organization).

The topic you suggest is quite satisfactory and I/(employer's name) look(s) forward to taking part in the program.

When you have completed your plans, please let us/me know the exact time to be at the (place).

Cordially,

b. Declining Topic

The topic you suggest is quite satisfactory, but I/(employer's name) would prefer to talk on (subject) if that is okay with you.

c. Requesting Topic

Do you have any preferences as to subject matter? Your suggestions would be welcome.

d. Suggesting Topic

(Topic) is a topic which would suit the occasion, don't you agree?

INVITATIONS, DECLINING

(1) Dinner or Luncheon

Dear _____:

Thank you for your dinner/luncheon invitation for (day of week) the (date).
I/(employer's name) regret(s) that I/(s)he can't make it because of a previous engagement/full schedule/business trip at that time.
Why don't you try me/us again sometime soon?

Cordially,

(2) Meeting, Party, Reception

Dear _____:

Thank you very much for your invitation to join the (name of organization) at the (place) on (date).
I/(employer's name) shall/will be unable to be

there at that time because of a <u>previous engagement/</u>
<u>full schedule/business trip</u>.

Accept my/our regrets. It would have been a
pleasure.

Cordially,

(3) Speechmaking

a. Straight Turndown

Dear _____ :

Thank you for asking <u>me</u>/<u>(employer's name)</u> to be
guest speaker at the (name) <u>breakfast/luncheon/din-</u>
<u>ner/meeting</u> or the (organization) at (place).

Because of a <u>previous engagement/full schedule/</u>
<u>business trip</u>, <u>I/(employer's name)</u> can't make it at
that time.

<u>Accept our/my regrets. It would have been a</u>
<u>pleasure</u>.

Sincerely,

b. Turndown with Offer of Substitute

<u>I/we would like to suggest, however, that a</u>
<u>close associate, (name), would make an excellent</u>
<u>speaker for your gathering. Call us/me if you are</u>
<u>interested</u>.

INVITATIONS, EXTENDING

(1) Dinner, Luncheon

Dear _____ :

Are you free for <u>dinner/lunch</u> or (day) of <u>this/</u>
<u>next</u> week, the (date)? If you are, <u>I/(employer's</u>
<u>name)</u> would like it so much if you could join <u>me/</u>
<u>him/her</u> at about (time) at (place).

This will give <u>us/you</u> an opportunity to talk
about (subject) and exchange views. Do let <u>me/us</u>
know if you can make it.

Cordially,

(2) Meeting

Dear _____ :

  As (employer's title) it would give <u>me</u>/<u>(employer's name)</u> great pleasure to have your presence at a meeting of (department, organization, group) scheduled for (date) at (place) to discuss (subject).

  Your thinking on the subject would contribute greatly to the success of the conference. Do let <u>me</u>/<u>us</u> know if you can make it.

Cordially,

(3) Party

Dear _____ :

  On (day of week) (date), (name of person, department, or organization) will celebrate (description of occasion).

  We have decided to have a party in honor of the occasion. The place is (name) on (address), and the time is (time). Come and bring your <u>husband</u>/<u>wife</u>/<u>boy friend</u>/<u>girl friend</u> or other guest. We look forward to seeing you.

  In order to make proper reservations, will you send your acceptance to the attention of (name of person) no later than (day, date)?

Cordially,

(4) Reception

Dear _____ :

  As (employer's title) it would give <u>me</u>/<u>(employer's name)</u> great pleasure to have your presence at a reception in honor of (name of person or event).

  The reception will be held in the (place), (address), on (day, time, date). Cocktails will be served promptly at (time), to be followed by <u>dinner</u>/<u>luncheon</u>/<u>a buffet</u> at (time). It will be <u>informal</u>/<u>semi-formal</u>/<u>formal</u>.

  <u>I</u>/<u>we</u> sincerely hope you can attend. Let <u>me</u>/<u>us</u> know.

Sincerely,

(5) Speechmaking

Dear _____:

    The (name of organization) would like to extend
to you an invitation to be our guest speaker on
(date) at the (description) <u>dinner/luncheon</u> to be
held at the (place) (address), at (time).

    As you know, the (organization) is interested
in (subject or subjects). Since you are familiar
with the field, we know your views will be extremely
interesting to us.

    You will receive further details later, but we
would appreciate having your acceptance soon so we
may complete our agenda.

Cordially,

ORDERS, CONFIRMING

(1) Placement of Employer's

Dear _____:

    This will confirm our order for (number) (name
of item) (description) at (price).

    We understand we will receive delivery of <u>this/
these</u> (name of item or items) on (date) at (place).

    Thank you for your prompt attention.

Sincerely,

(2) Receipt of Another's

Dear _____:

    This will confirm your order for (number, quan-
tity, amount) (name of item) (description) at
(price).

    You will receive delivery of <u>this/these</u> (name
of item or items) on (date) at (place).

    Thank you for your patronage.

Cordially,

PART TWO

Letters Usually Signed by Employer

Chapter A ADJUSTMENTS TO ANNOUNCEMENTS

Contents

ADJUSTMENTS OF COMPLAINTS

(1) Billing Claimed Incorrect

a. Amount of Bill Incorrect

Dear _____:

  Thank you for calling our attention to the error in your account.
  <u>The amount has been corrected and a revised bill is enclosed/will be sent to you shortly.</u>
  Please accept our apologies.

Cordially,

b. Bill for Goods Not Ordered

  <u>The charge of (amount) for a shipment of (product) was due to a clerical error, and a credit memo is enclosed/will be sent to you shortly.</u>

c. Bill for Merchandise Returned

  <u>Evidently your bill was processed before the return was recorded. Kindly ignore the incorrect charge.</u>

(2) Product Unsatisfactory

a. Pick-Up for Replacement, Credit, or Refund

Dear _____:

  We are very sorry to learn that the (name of product) you purchased has not proved satisfactory.

We want our customers to be happy with our merchandise, and thank you for bringing the matter to our attention.

Will you kindly let us know the time and day when it will be convenient to have this (product) picked up and returned? Also, will you inform us whether you wish to receive a replacement, a credit, or a cash refund?

We regret the inconvenience caused you, and hope to continue to serve you in the future.

Cordially,

b. Return for Replacement, Credit, or Refund

If you wish to return the (product) to us for a replacement, a credit, or cash refund, kindly let us know and we will be happy to accommodate you.

(3) Service Unsatisfactory

Dear _____:

We sincerely regret the unsatisfactory service you received from one of our attendants/employees/operators/repairmen/salesclerks recently.

As a patron of our establishment, you should know that such service is not customary. Through careful selection and supervision of our employees we try to see that our customers are taken care of efficiently and courteously at all times. When this is not the case, we appreciate having the matter called to our attention.

Thank you for taking the time to write us, and we shall try even harder in future to give you the kind of service you expect.

Sincerely,

(4) Shipment Delayed, Incorrect, Incomplete

    a. Delayed

Dear _____:

    We are sorry for the <u>delay/error</u> in our ship-
ment to you of (name of product).
    <u>Due to some unexpected problems, the order</u>
<u>could not be filled/shipped as promptly as we had</u>
<u>hoped. We trust this has not caused you too much in-</u>
<u>convenience, and assure you it will not happen</u>
<u>again.</u>
    Thank you for your patience.

Sincerely,

    b. Incorrect, Incomplete

    <u>A replacement is being sent you for the items</u>
<u>that failed to reach you/were sent in error, and we</u>
<u>hope that your order has now been filled to your</u>
<u>satisfaction.</u>

AGREEMENTS AND CONTRACTS

(1) Confirmation of Verbal Job Agreement

Dear _____:

    This will confirm the arrangement made (date)
in connection with the position of (name of position) here at (name of company), starting on (date).

1. The job will carry the title: (title)
2. The duties entail (description of duties)
3. The beginning salary is (amount) per <u>week/month/</u>
   <u>year</u>.
4. There will be a <u>secretary/assistant/(other)</u> as-
   signed to help you.

(Items 5 and 6 for salesmen)

5. There will be a car allowance of (amount) per

month, plus (amount) per mile for car travel on company business.
6. There is a (percentage) commission on company sales over and above (amount).

I'm/<u>We're</u> sure you'll enjoy your work at (name of company), and <u>I'm/we're</u> delighted to know you'll be with us shortly.

Cordially,

(2) Informal Contract

Dear _____:

This letter will constitute an agreement be-tween you and (name of person(s) or company(ies) with regard to the (kind of work) you are to do for us.
1. You agree to (description of work to be done).
2. You are to start as of (date) and conclude on or before (date).
3. For this work you are to be paid the sum of (amount) of which (amount) is to be paid on sign-ing of this agreement, and (amount) <u>monthly/week-ly/daily/yearly/at the satisfactory conclusion of the assignment</u>.

Please sign all copies of this letter and re-turn them to me. I will have them processed and return a copy to you with a check for the initial payment.

Sincerely,

(signature)

_____
(addressee's signature)

_____
(signature of other
party to agreement)

ANNOUNCEMENTS OF IMPORTANCE

(1) Merger of Business

Dear _____:

    Effective on (date), the (name) Company will become associated with the (name) organization. This merger gives added strength to (name) both in terms of public acceptance and operative capital, and we hope to be able to serve you more promptly and efficiently than ever before.

    I'm/We're sure you'll be pleased that all/most of your old friends at (name) will remain on the staff since the new owners don't want to disturb relationships that have been built up over the years.

Cordially,

(2) New Employee Introduction

Dear _____:

    It is with pleasure that I/we inform you that effective (date), (name) will join our staff. (Name) comes from a background of (description), and his/her most recent connection was with the (name) company. (Name) is extremely personable, as well as highly capable.

    Whenever he/she gets in touch with you, I/we know I/we can count on your usual cooperation.

Cordially,

(3) New Location of Office

Dear _____:

    In keeping with our increased size/prestige, the (name) Company moved to a new location on (date). The new site is also more convenient to transportation/parking facilities.

Why not drop in sometime after the (date) and let <u>me</u>/<u>us</u> show you around? You'll probably be interested in the new (name) <u>department</u>/<u>system</u>/<u>machinery</u>/<u>equipment</u>/<u>division</u> we've now added.

Cordially,

(4) New Telephone Number

a. Additional Number

Dear _____:

In order to serve you better, we have obtained an additional telephone number, (number), which you may dial when our old number is busy. <u>I</u>/<u>we</u> hope this will contribute to our efficiency and promptness when doing business with you.

Cordially,

b. New Location

Dear _____:

Due to our recent change in location, our telephone number has now been changed to (number). If you will make note of this in your records, it will save you time and trouble in calling us.

Cordially,

(5) Promotion of Employee

Dear _____:

It is a pleasure to write this letter telling you that effective (date), (name) will be promoted to the position of (name of position). (Name) has been with the (name) Company for (number) years in the capacity of (position), and has proven to be extremely capable.

<u>He</u>/<u>She</u> will probably be in touch with you shortly, and <u>I</u>/<u>we</u> know you will find the contact rewarding.

Cordially,

(6) Rate Increases for Service

Dear _____:

    Effective on (date), there will be a slight
increase in (name of service) rates, necessitated
by a continuing rise in costs. A copy of our rate
card, giving full information, is enclosed.

    I/We am/are sure that this modest increase will
be more than offset by the improved service we offer, and we will continue to give you more for your
money than our competitors.

Cordially,

(7) Resignation, Retirement, or Transferral of Official

    a. Resignation

Dear _____:

    Like most of our clients/customers/friends, you
probably/perhaps don't know that on (date), (name),
our (name of position) will no longer be with the
(name) branch/department of (name) Company.

    (Name has been with us for (number) years and
made many friends in the business. While we wish
him/her well in his/her new career elsewhere,
(name)'s presence here will, we are sure, be sorely
missed.

    We are, however, completely confident that your
needs will be served most competently by our new
(name of position), (name of person), whose background in the field covers (number) years.

Cordially,

    b. Retirement

    (Name) has been with us for (number) years and
made many friends in the business. While certainly
entitled to a life of leisure, he/she will, we are
sure, be sorely missed.

c. Transferral

(Name) has been with us for (number) years and made many friends in the business. While we wish him/her well as (title) in the (name) branch/department, (name)'s presence here will, we are sure, be sorely missed.

Chapter B   BANQUETS
AND BILLING

Contents

BANQUETS

(1) Accepting Invitations

Dear _____:

It is very kind of you to want me as your guest at the (name of organization) banquet on (date) at the (place).

It will be most interesting and informative to hear (name of speaker or speakers). I am familiar with his/her/their work and look forward to hearing his/her/their views on (subject).

I'll be at the (place) at (time) and will look for you there.

Cordially,

(2) Arranging

Dear _____:

This organization has completed plans to hold its (name) convention/meeting at the (place) on (date). I wish to arrange for a banquet on the evening of (date), with an attendance of approximately (number).

Will you estimate for me what it will cost to serve a first-class dinner in the (name) Room for (number) people? Your price should include (number) cocktails per person. I'd like you to send me several menu suggestions so that I may make a selection.

I hope you can give this your immediate attention so that I can notify the prospective guests promptly.

Sincerely,

(3) Declining Invitation

Dear _____:

Thank you very much for your invitation to join the (name of organization) at your banquet on (date) at the (place).

Unfortunately, I am unable to be there at that time because of a previous engagement/full schedule/ business trip. It would have been a pleasure to see you and to hear (name of speaker or speakers).

Please accept my regrets.

Cordially,

(4) Extending Invitation

Dear _____:

As a person with an interest in (subject), I think you'd enjoy hearing the speaker(s), (name or names), at the (name of organization) banquet on (date) at (place).

If this sounds good to you, won't you be our guest that evening? Cocktails will be served at (time), with dinner about (time). The after-dinner speakers are no doubt known to you as (occupation) in (field).

If you can join us, won't you let me know?

Cordially,

BILLING

(1) Correcting Bills Received

Dear _____:

We have not paid your bill for the (date) shipment of (product or goods), because it was for a

different amount than the price of the merchandise
we received. We ordered only (amount or number) of
(product or goods) at (price), which would come to
(amount) according to our figures.

Therefore, we would appreciate your sending us
a corrected bill, which we will pay immediately on
receipt.

Sincerely,

(2) Correcting Bills Sent

Dear _____:

To answer your letter of (date), the invoice
for the merchandise shipped you on (date) will be
corrected to (amount), instead of (amount) in accordance with your request.

I/We regret this clerical error, and assure you
it will not happen again.

Sincerely,

(3) Covering Letter with Bill

Dear _____:

Enclosed is our bill for (amount) for (number)
(name of product) purchased by you on (date).

We will expect payment within (number) days,
according to our usual terms.

Thank you for your patronage.

Sincerely,

(4) Explaining Payment Plan

    a. Charge Account

Dear _____:

We feel sure you would like to bring your
charge account up-to-date by reducing the outstanding sum you owe us. This amount of (amount) can be

paid in installments if you would find that more
convenient.

You may pay off the bill at the rate of
(amount) a month over a period of (number) months.
The carrying charges will amount to only (amount) a
month, which can be added to each monthly payment.
Just stop at the credit desk, or send us a check
or money order to make your first partial payment
on the bill. Then use your charge account, as usual,
for additional purchases.

We hope to see you or hear from you very soon.

Cordially,

b. Confirmation of Costs

Dear _____:

This will confirm our mutual agreement to start
on the (description of work to be done) as soon as
possible. The work will conform to the specifications as approved by you (date).

For your records, the total cost will be
(amount). (Number) percent of this amount must be
paid as soon as possible so that we may begin. Another (number) percent will be due on (date). The
balance is payable on full completion of the entire
project. A cost sheet is attached. If we can place
our order for materials by (date), work can start
on or before (date).

I/We look forward to this opportunity to serve
you.

Sincerely,

(5) Requesting Confirmation of Payment Plan

a. Discount

Dear _____:

Yesterday I/we received your invoice #(number),
dated (date), in the amount of (amount). It is my/

<u>our</u> understanding that the (name of item) <u>I/we</u>
bought from you would be billed at a (number) percent discount. Will you please ask your billing department, therefore, to cancel this invoice and
issue a new one in the proper amount?

Sincerely,

b. Interest

Dear _____:

    <u>Yesterday/Today/A few days ago</u> <u>I/we</u> received
your invoice #(number), dated (date), in the amount
of (amount).
    It is <u>my/our</u> understanding that the install-
ments on the (name of item) <u>I/we</u> bought from you
would be billed at a (number) percent interest rate.
Will you kindly confirm this, and ask your billing
department to cancel this invoice and issue a new
one in the proper amount of (amount)?

Sincerely,

Chapter C CANCELLATIONS THROUGH CREDIT ARRANGEMENTS

Contents

Cancellations

Collection Letters

Complaints, Adjusting

Complaints, Making

Condolence

Confirmations

Congratulations Offered

Contracts

Conventions

Covering Letters

With Bill (see Billing B)
Others (see Enclosures E)

Credit Arrangements

Charge Accounts, Opening
Loss of Credit
Payment Deadline
References, Requesting
          Supplying
Refusing Credit

CANCELLATIONS

(1) Cancelling Appointments

Dear _____:

The prospect of visiting with you at (place) on (date) was a very pleasant one, and I had looked forward to it with interest. That's why I'm extremely sorry to tell you that I will be unable to keep the appointment, due to an <u>illness in the family</u>/<u>unexpected emergency</u>.

At present, I don't know when I will return to my desk, but if you'll check in a <u>few days</u>/<u>week</u>/<u>couple of weeks</u>, my secretary will set up another appointment at your convenience.

Cordially,

(2) Cancelling Orders

Dear _____:

Due to a change in plans, we will no longer be able to use the (name of product or service) we ordered from you on (date).

Will you, therefore, cancel our order. We will be in touch with you again when we are in the market for (name of product or service).

Thank you very much, and we regret any inconvenience we may have caused.

Sincerely,

COLLECTION LETTERS

(1) General Delinquency

Dear _____:

    In looking over your account, we note that there still remains a balance of (amount) now overdue for (number) <u>days/weeks/months</u>.
    We will appreciate, therefore, receiving your remittance in the sum of (amount) within the next <u>few days/week/ten days/two weeks</u>.
    If your remittance has already been sent, please accept our thanks and disregard this letter.

Cordially,

(2) New Customer Delinquency

Dear _____:

    We hope that you have enjoyed <u>shopping at our store</u>/<u>using our services</u>/<u>using our product(s)</u>.
    However, we've noticed that as of this writing we haven't received payment in the amount of (amount) still outstanding on your account. If there was something wrong with the <u>merchandise/service</u>, or a question about the bill, please let us know.
    If it has simply slipped your mind, just attach your check or money order to this letter and return it in the next mail.

Cordially,

(3) Old Customer Delinquency

    a. Balance Past Due

Dear _____:

    With every assurance that you will understand <u>my/our</u> motives, <u>I/we</u> want to bring to your attention something that concerns us both.
    <u>An examination of your account indicates that the balance is past due. I/We appreciate the fine</u>

relationship we have long enjoyed, but at the same
time it is important that your payments be received
according to our terms.

If your current payment is late because of some
problems you are having, I/we will be glad to discuss it. However, if the delay is inadvertent, I/we
wish you would check into it and see that we receive
an early remittance. Thanks a lot.

Sincerely,

b. Continued Delinquency

Our records show that your payments are reaching us late with increasing regularity. I/We appreciate your business, but at the same time I/we would
like to receive your payments when they are due.

c. Itemized Listing

I/We appreciate the fine relationship we have
long enjoyed, but an analysis of your account indicates that the balance listed below is past due:
(make itemized list)

(4) Series of Letters (Appeals, Inquiries, Reminders, Threats)

a. Appeal to Fairness

Dear _____:

We are sorry that we must call your attention
to your unpaid balance of (amount) which has been
past due since (time).

Your account was opened with the understanding
that we would do our best to serve you, while you in
turn would make payment in accordance with our terms.
Since we have carried out our part of the agreement,
we think it only fair to expect that you live up to
yours.

Please send us your check for (amount) at once.

Sincerely,

b. Inquiry as to Reason

If there is some reason why payment has not been made, we should appreciate your letting us know. Otherwise, we shall assume that nonpayment is due to an oversight which you will now correct.

c. Reminder

This is intended as a friendly reminder, and now that it has again been brought to your notice, we are sure you will want to bring your account up-to-date.

d Threat of Legal Action

We have repeatedly brought this matter to your attention and we are disappointed to have received no cooperation. Although we do not like to resort to legal action, it seems to be our only recourse. Unless we receive full payment by (date) we shall be forced to turn this account over to our attorneys.

COMPLAINTS, MAKING

(1) Product Unsatisfactory

a. Damaged

Dear _____:

On (date) we received our shipment of (product) ordered from you on (date).
We are sorry to report that the (product) was/were damaged en route, and is/are no longer in condition for use/resale.
Kindly let us know what disposal you wish us to make of the (product), and how soon we may expect a replacement/reimbursement.

Sincerely,

b. Defective

<u>We are sorry to report that the (product) is/</u>
<u>are defective, due to (description of defect), and</u>
<u>consequently impossible for us to use/sell.</u>

(2) Service Unsatisfactory

Dear _____:

On (date) we made use of your (description)
service.
We are sorry to report that the service was unsatisfactory, and wish to register the following
complaint:
(complaint)
Kindly let us know whether we may expect you to
complete the work to our satisfaction or reduce the
amount of your bill accordingly.

Sincerely,

(3) Shipment Delayed, Incorrect

a. Delayed

Dear _____:

On (date) we ordered from you (product) to be
delivered on (date).
<u>The shipment has not yet arrived, and every</u>
<u>day's delay means loss/inconvenience for us. If the</u>
<u>(product) is/are en route, please telephone us when</u>
<u>to expect it/them. If the order has not yet been</u>
<u>sent out, we would appreciate your putting a rush on</u>
<u>it. If the order has been held up because it/part of</u>
<u>it is presently unavailable, kindly inform us.</u>
Please let us hear from you immediately.

Sincerely,

b. Incorrect

The shipment arrived on time, but in the wrong
quantity/model/style/color/size. Kindly advise when/
how you plan to correct/complete the order.

CONFIRMATIONS

(1) Costs of Product or Service

a. Product

Dear _____:

In our discussion on (date) I/you expressed
interest in your/our (name of product or service).
This will confirm the offer of (number) (description) (product or products) at a price of
(amount), to be delivered by (date).
Will you please send me written confirmation
of your acceptance of this order/offer?

Cordially,

b. Service

This will confirm the offer of (amount) to do
the (description) job in question, which will be
started on (day and/or hour) and concluded on (day
and/or hour).

(2) Payment, Method

Dear _____:

This will confirm our mutual agreement as to
method of payment for (description of product or
service).
For your records, the total cost will be
(amount). (Number) percent of this amount must be
paid (date), so that we may proceed promptly. Another (number) percent will be due on (date). The
balance is payable on (date or dates).
We look forward to serving you.

Sincerely,

(3) Program to be Followed

Dear _____:

This will confirm our mutual agreement in connection with the (name) program.

For your records, (description) work is to be begun on (date), and proceed as discussed, reaching (description) point about (date) and conclusion on or about (date).

I/We trust this is satisfactory.

Cordially,

(4) Salary, Amount

Dear _____:

This will confirm the arrangement made (date) in connection with the position of (name of job) here at (name of company).

The job will pay (amount) per week/month/year to start. There will be, provided your work is satisfactory, an opportunity for increase at the end of a (time) period. Hospitalization/Life insurance/Pension plan(s) is/are available after (length of time).

We'll expect you at (time) on (day, date). We look forward to your arrival.

Cordially,

(5) Shipping Charges

Dear _____:

This will confirm my/our quotation to you of (amount) for (number) (description) (product).

If we use air freight, the price for shipment will be (amount). Shipment by surface would cost only (amount), but delivery will be slower.

If you wish to authorize immediate shipment by either method, please let me/us know promptly. Thank you for your interest.

Cordially,

CONGRATULATIONS OFFERED

(1) Achievement, Business

Dear _____:

    Only a brief message to congratulate you on the excellent record you made in (month or year).

    Your <u>efficiency/production/sales</u> report has just been received. The (name) <u>branch/department/ division/section</u>, as you undoubtedly know, was tops in the area of <u>production/cost savings/sales</u>. It is entirely due to the loyalty and tireless effort of the <u>department head/entire department/production chief/sales chief/sales department</u> that such achievements are possible.

    Keep up the good work, (name).

Cordially,

(2) New Job

Dear _____:

    Just a note to let you know how pleased I was to hear of your new appointment. I'm sure that your proven capability in the field of (name of field) will be just what the (name) Company needs.

    Best wishes for your success in the job.

Cordially,

(3) Promotion, Business

Dear _____:

    I know how happy you and (wife's name) must be at the news of your promotion. You've worked hard, (name), and the new title is well deserved.

    My very best wishes to you.

Cordially,

CONVENTIONS

(1) Accepting Invitations

Dear _____:

    Thank you for your invitation to attend the (name) Convention to be held in (place) the week of (date).

    I am happy to have our store/company/organization represented, and I am enclosing my reservation form.

    See you in (place).

Sincerely,

(2) Declining Invitations

    a. Completely

Dear _____:

    Thank you for your invitation to attend the (name) Convention to be held in (place) the week of (date). I had hoped that it would be possible for me to be there, but I now find the rush of business makes it impractical.

    Please accept my regrets, and I'll try to make it next year.

Cordially,

    b. With Suggested Substitute

    However, I want our organization to be represented, so I have asked my co-worker (name) to take my place. He/She is looking forward to the opportunity to attend.

(2) Extending Invitations

Dear _____:

    We hope you have set aside the week of (date)

in order to attend the (name) Convention to be held
in (place) this year.

The seminars will be held at the (place) and
sessions will start each morning at (time) in the
(name) Room. Lunch will be served in the (location)
from (time) until (time). After (time) you are free
for relaxation, and evening entertainment has been
arranged.

The cost of the entire (period), including
transportation by (name) Airlines from (place) to
(place), will be (amount). Planes will leave (name)
Airport on (date) at (time). If you are interested,
please fill in the attached reservation form and return it to me/us. No reservations will be accepted
after (date).

I/We know you will find your stay enjoyable as
well as productive, and look forward to seeing you.

Cordially,

CREDIT ARRANGEMENTS

(1) Charge Accounts, Opening

Dear _____:

We are pleased to send you the enclosed credit
card/charge plate, in accordance with your request.
Will you kindly sign the card/plate at once?

Unless otherwise instructed, we will bill you
on a monthly calendar basis with a 30-day charge,
without interest, on any item purchased. If you
would prefer our delayed payment plan which bills
you for (amount) percent of your outstanding balance
each month, there is an interest charge of (amount)
percent a month on the balance each billing date.

Thank you for your patronage.

Sincerely,

(2) Loss of Credit

Dear _____:

    Your account, as shown on the enclosed statement, indicates (number) items long past due. Since the balance on your account will soon amount to (amount), we feel that we must stop extending you credit until your current obligation of (amount) is paid.

    We regret the necessity for taking this action, but we think you will understand that we cannot continue to carry this outstanding indebtedness indefinitely.

Sincerely,

(3) Payment Deadline

Dear _____:

    Enclosed is our (date) statement carrying a notation that no further purchases can be delivered to you until we receive full payment of our (date or dates) billings.

    Since your credit standing is good, it is difficult to understand why the (amount) has been on our books since (date). We hope you can see your way clear to letting us have a check by next (date) in full/partial payment, so that we can get the matter cleared up soon.

Sincerely,

(4) Reference, Requesting from Bank

Dear _____:

    (Name), who has applied for a charge account with us, has told us that (s)he has a checking account with you.

    We should appreciate your letting us know how

long (name) has had the account and how much <u>his/</u>
<u>her</u> balances customarily average.

Sincerely,

(5) Reference, Supplying

Dear _____:

    Our credit department tells me that our experi-
ence with (name) has been <u>excellent/unsatisfactory</u>.
<u>He/She/They</u> pay(s) <u>promptly/slowly</u>, and we have had
<u>no trouble/trouble</u> effecting settlement of the ac-
count since it was first opened on (date).
    On the strength of these facts, I feel you
<u>will/will not</u> be justified in extending credit to
(name).

Sincerely,

(6) Refusing Credit

a. Previous Payment Difficulties

Dear _____:

    It is gratifying to know from your recent ap-
plication for a credit account that we have earned
your good opinion. We hope we may always enjoy your
confidence and approval.
    <u>In accordance with our policy, we have care-</u>
<u>fully investigated the references you provided.</u>
<u>While, in most respects, your past record is satis-</u>
<u>factory, there has been a pattern of periodic pay-</u>
<u>ment difficulties.</u>
    Although we cannot extend credit privileges
at the present time, we would be happy to ship merchandise to you on C.O.D. terms. Perhaps in the future, if you try us again, we may be able to recon-
sider your application.
    Meanwhile, we hope you will give us the oppor-
tunity to serve you.

Sincerely,

b. Unsatisfactory Credit Information

To our regret, however, we find that current credit information available to us does not provide a sufficient basis for establishing an account for you now.

Chapter D DECISIONS THROUGH DISMISSALS

Contents

DECISIONS AND OPINIONS

(1) Expressing Opinions on a Person

    a. Negative

Dear _____:

    I have your request of (date) for an endorsement in connection with the candidacy of (name) for (office).

    <u>Frankly, I do not think I shall cast my vote for (name). This is certainly not a personal rejection. It merely means that I prefer the platform of one of (name's) opponents.</u>

    In any case, I am sure the majority of the vote will go to the most deserving candidate.

Sincerely,

    b. Positive

    <u>Frankly, I am happy to make a statement in favor of (name's) candidacy, as I consider him/her eminently qualified to carry out the duties of (office) in a way that will benefit everyone. (Name's) stands on the issues which concern us should assure good leadership for the city/county/state/nation/ organization upon his election.</u>

c. Undecided

<u>Frankly, I am still uncertain how I shall cast</u>
<u>my vote, and I need a little time to decide which of</u>
<u>the candidates has the most appeal for me. I am sure</u>
<u>(name) will agree with my decision not to offer an</u>
<u>endorsement until I am sure of my own opinion. Why</u>
<u>don't you get in touch with me in another few days/</u>
<u>weeks/months, when I have considered the matter</u>
<u>further</u>?

(2) Making Decisions on a Subject

Dear _____:

In reply to your request of (date) that I make
a decision about (subject), I <u>am</u>/<u>am not</u> in favor of
the <u>drive</u>/<u>movement</u>/<u>proposition</u>/<u>idea</u>/<u>amendment</u>, and
<u>would</u>/<u>would not</u> agree to work personally in its
support.
Thank you for thinking of me in this connection. I appreciate your confidence in my judgment.

Cordially,

(3) Requesting Decisions or Support

Dear _____:

The (organization) is at present making plans
to back the (description) <u>drive</u>/<u>movement</u>/<u>proposi-</u>
<u>tion</u>/<u>idea</u>/<u>amendment</u>, and would like to enlist your
personal support.
We would appreciate learning your feelings on
the subject, and your active cooperation would be
helpful. It will facilitate matters if you can let
us have your decision by the (date).

Cordially,

(4) Requesting Opinions or Endorsement

Dear _____:

    Your name has been given <u>me/us</u> by (name) with
the suggestions that <u>I/we</u> request an endorsement by
you for (name) as a candidate for (office) <u>in/at/
of</u> (place).
    (Name's) program for the <u>city/county/state/na-
tion/organization</u> should, <u>I am/we are</u> sure, be of
benefit to us all, if <u>his/her</u> past record is any
indication.
    Any statement you care to make in <u>his/her</u> be-
half will be greatly appreciated.

Cordially,

DELAYS, EXPLAINING

(1) Acknowledging Invitations

    a. Accepting

Dear _____:
    Please accept my apologies for the delay in
acknowledging your invitation for <u>lunch/dinner/cock-
tails</u> on (date). I have been away from the office
and only just returned.
    <u>Luckily, I have no other plans for the date you
mention, and shall be happy to see you at (time) at
(place)</u>.

Cordially,

    b. Declining

    <u>Unfortunately, I have other plans for the date
you mention, but shall be happy to make a date for
some other convenient time</u>.

(2) Filling Orders

a. Executive's Absence

Dear _____:

This will acknowledge receipt of your order of (date) for (type of merchandise or service).

Although I have been away from the office, I processed your order immediately upon my return.

I do hope the delay has not caused you any inconvenience, and wish to assure you that your patronage is appreciated.

Cordially,

b. Manpower or Production Difficulties

Due to some temporary personnel/production/delivery problems, your order could not be taken care of until now.

(3) Making Purchases

Dear _____:

Since I have been out of town, my staff delayed making our purchase of (name of equipment/material/service/supply), waiting for authorization from me.

If you will fill the enclosed order at your earliest convenience, I shall appreciate it very much.

Cordially,

(4) Replying to Inquiry

Dear _____:

Thank you for your recent inquiry about our products/services/procedures/prices.

We wish to apologize for the inadvertent delay

in giving you the desired information, which we
<u>enclose herewith</u>/<u>itemize below</u>.

    We appreciate your interest, and hope to hear
from you further.

Cordially,

DISMISSAL ANNOUNCEMENT
(AGENT, EMPLOYEE, SALES REPRESENTATIVE)

Dear   :

    (Name) will no longer be <u>working with</u>/<u>repre-</u>
<u>senting</u> us after (date). (S)He leaves with our best
wishes for future success.

    In a few days <u>I</u>/<u>we</u> will be in touch with you to
introduce (name's) replacement. In the meantime,
feel free to call on <u>me</u>/<u>us</u>, if there is anything <u>I</u>/
<u>we</u> can do to serve you.

Cordially,

Chapter E   ENCLOSURES
AND ERRORS

Contents

ENCLOSURES OR COVERING LETTERS

(1) Descriptive or Explanatory

Dear _____:

We are happy to send you our <u>circular</u>/<u>booklet</u>/ <u>catalog</u>/<u>price list</u>/<u>estimate</u>, which you requested on (date).

Our (name) department has provided this material which describes our <u>products</u>/<u>prices</u>/<u>services</u> in detail. We hope that you will find the enclosure helpful in making your <u>selection</u>/<u>decision</u>.

It is always a pleasure to serve you.

Sincerely,

(2) Transmitting without Comment

Dear _____:

The attached <u>circular</u>/<u>booklet</u>/<u>catalog</u>/<u>price list</u>/<u>photograph</u>/<u>document</u>/<u>statement</u> is enclosed for your purposes in connection with (subject).

We hope you will find it useful, and we will be happy to hear from you again at any time.

Cordially,

ERRORS IN ACCOUNTS

(1) Making Correction of Mistake—Theirs

a. New Bill

Dear _____:

In accordance with your instructions, we are returning your invoice No. (number), dated (date), for (amount), representing the purchase of (item or items) on (date or dates).

We understand that you will issue us a corrected bill in the amount of (amount), and we will be happy to make payment upon its receipt.

Cordially,

b. No Bill

We understand that you will now make the necessary correction in our account, and we appreciate your cooperation.

(2) Making correction of Mistake—Yours

a. New Bill

Dear _____:

Thank you for returning our invoice No. (number), dated (date), for (amount), so that we may make the necessary correction in your account.

Enclosed is a new invoice in the amount of (amount). We are sorry for the error/misunderstanding and appreciate your calling it to our attention.

Sincerely,

b. No Bill

We are sorry for the error/misunderstanding and appreciate your calling it to our attention.

(3) Requesting Correction of Mistake—Theirs

a. Clerical Error

Dear _____:

We have just received you invoice No. (number), dated (date), amounting to (amount), representing the purchase of (item or items, service or services) on (date or dates).

Our records show the amount due for this purchase/service to be (amount). We assume that the

<u>figure on your invoice is a clerical error.</u>
    The invoice is being returned to you herewith
for correction.

Sincerely,

b. Credit Due

<u>Your records should show that we had a credit</u>
<u>due us of (amount). This would reduce the amount</u>
<u>owed to (amount).</u>

c. Misunderstanding on Price

<u>We understood that we were to be billed at a</u>
<u>discount/wholesale/reduced price. According to those</u>
<u>terms the amount owed would be only (amount).</u>

(4) Requesting Correction of Mistake—Yours

a. Clerical Error

Dear _____:

    We recently sent you our invoice No. (number),
dated (date), amounting to (amount), representing
the purchase of (item or items, service or services)
on (date or dates).
    <u>Since then, a check of our records indicates</u>
<u>that, due to a clerical error, the figures on your</u>
<u>invoice are incorrect.</u>
    If you will return the invoice to us, we will
make the necessary correction.

Cordially,

b. Credit Due

    <u>Since then, a check of our records indicates</u>
<u>that you have a credit due you of (amount). This</u>
<u>would reduce the amount owed us to (amount).</u>

c. Misunderstanding on Price

    <u>Since then, a check of our records indicates</u>
<u>that you were to be billed at a discount/wholesale/</u>
<u>reduced price. According to those terms the amount</u>
<u>owed would be only (amount).</u>

Chapter F   FOLLOW-UPS
Contents

Follow-ups

FOLLOW-UPS

(1) Reminders of Dates Made

Dear _____:

    This is a reminder that we have a <u>luncheon/meeting</u> scheduled at (place) for (date) at (time). Since we made the date some time ago, I thought I'd jog your memory.

    I look forward to seeing you then, as I am sure we will have much to discuss.

Cordially,

(2) Unanswered Letters

Dear _____:

    In examining my follow-up file today, I notice that I have not received a reply to my letter to you dated (date), concerning (subject). In case the letter has gone astray or been mislaid, I enclose a copy for your information.

    I look forward to hearing from you soon, as I am anxious to have your reactions to my <u>idea(s)/suggestion(s)/recommendation(s)</u>.

Cordially,

(3) Unreturned Phone Calls

Dear _____:

On examining my calendar today, I notice that I have not received a reply to my phone call to you on (date), when I wanted to discuss (subject). In case my message has been mislaid, or you've just forgotten to return the call, I'm bringing the matter to your attention now.

I look forward to hearing from you soon, as I think an exchange of ideas would be helpful to us both.

Cordially,

Chapter G   GOOD WILL

Contents

Good Will

GOOD WILL

(1) Appreciation to Customer or Associate (Seasonal)

Dear _____:

    As the <u>holiday season begins</u>/<u>New Year ap-</u><u>proaches</u>/<u>summer season starts</u>, <u>I</u>/<u>we</u> can't help but appreciate how much more enjoyable it will be, due to the knowledge that we can count (name of company or person) among our <u>friends</u>/<u>customers</u>/<u>associates</u>.

    Our relationship with you has always been one of understanding and cooperation. After doing busi-ness with you for (period) <u>I</u>/<u>we</u> have come to believe that you are one of the finest <u>concerns</u>/<u>outfits</u>/<u>persons</u> in the field.

    If <u>our</u>/<u>my</u> expression of appreciation adds to your enjoyment of the <u>holidays</u>/<u>New Year</u>/<u>summer</u>, <u>I</u>/<u>we</u> will be well rewarded.

    Please accept <u>our</u>/<u>my</u> best wishes for you and yours for a happy <u>holiday</u>/<u>New Year</u>/<u>vacation</u>.

Sincerely,

(2) Birthday or Anniversary of Business Relationship

Dear _____:

    It gives <u>us</u>/<u>me</u> great pleasure to remind you that we have been doing business together for (num-ber) years. Such pleasant, long-standing relation-ships do not occur by chance. They reflect the mu-tual loyalty and confidence that have developed be-tween us over this period.

All of us here at the (name) Company wish to extend to you and your staff our heartiest thanks, and to wish you continued success in the years to come.

Sincerely,

(3) Thank You for Compliment, Favor, or Suggestion

a. Compliment

Dear _____:

Thank you very much for your kind letter of (date), concerning (subject).
It is always gratifying to receive a complimentary letter like yours, which indicates that our efforts to serve you are appreciated. You may be sure that our (name of person, department, division) will receive appropriate recognition for a job well done.
Thank you again for your courtesy.

Cordially,

b. Favor

It was good of you to come to my assistance, and I appreciate your generosity. Your aid will be invaluable in helping me accomplish my objectives. If I can reciprocate at any time, please be sure to call on me.

c. Suggestion

Your suggestion that we (content of suggestion) has been passed along to the appropriate department. You may be sure it will be given every consideration. As soon as we reach a conclusion, you will hear from us.

(4) Thank You to Old Employee (Seasonal)

Dear _____ :

In reviewing the events of the past year, it is apparent that the fact we go into (year) in such satisfactory condition is largely due to your excellent contribution.

I wish to extend my sincere thanks to you (name), for your efforts, and want to assure you that they will be suitably rewarded at the earliest possible moment.

Meanwhile, I would like to wish you and yours the best of everything in the year to come.

Cordially,

(5) Welcome to New Customer

Dear _____ :

It is a great pleasure to welcome your patronage of (name of Company). We hope to add your name to our list of satisfied customers/clients/guests.

We try to show our appreciation for the business we receive by providing your money's worth in service/quality/comfort.

It is our sincere wish to make your shopping/transactions/visit here as pleasant as possible.

We are ready and eager to serve you.

Cordially,

(6) Welcome to Prospective Customer

Dear _____ :

It gives us great pleasure to welcome you to the city of (name).

We are sure you will enjoy being here, and you

are cordially invited to visit with us when you have
the opportunity. We would like you to become famil-
iar with our <u>merchandise</u>/<u>service</u>/<u>facilities</u>, and our
friendly personnel will be glad to be of assistance.

    If there is anything we can do to make you feel
at home, don't hesitate to call on us.

Cordially,

(7) Welcome to New Employee

Dear _____:

    It is a great pleasure to welcome you, (name),
to our organization.

    The work you have done in (subject) at (place),
indicates that we are fortunate to have you joining
us at (company) as (position). You'll be working
with many congenial people, and I'm sure you'll find
them capable and cooperative.

    Let's get together for a chat, as soon as you
are settled. Meanwhile, if there is anything I can
do for you, just let me know.

Sincerely,

Chapter I INFORMATION THROUGH INTRODUCTIONS

Contents

INFORMATION

(1) Acknowledging Receipt

Dear _____:

    Thank you very much for sending us/me informa-
tion concerning (subject).

    I/We appreciate your putting this at our/my
disposal, as it should be extremely helpful. If at
any time I/we can reciprocate, don't hesitate to
call on me/us.

Cordially,

(2) Referral to a Better Source

Dear _____:

    I/We have your letter of (date) requesting in-
formation about (subject).

    As any data we may have on the subject is quite
limited, I/we would suggest you send an inquiry to
(name of person or company), who should be able to
give you full details.

    Thank you for thinking of us. We are always
happy to be of assistance.

Cordially,

(3) Requesting from Someone

Dear _____:

    I/We am/are interested in securing information
concerning (subject).

As your organization is one of the most promi-
nent in the field, I/we decided to turn to you for
assistance. If you have any material you think would
be helpful, I/we would appreciate your sending it
along.

Since our need is quite urgent, may we hear
from you soon?

Cordially,

(4) Supplying to Inquirer

Dear _____:

Thank you for your interest in our company.
We are/I am enclosing/sending separately the litera-
ture/statistics/prices/descriptive material/illus-
trations, which I/we think will serve your needs.

If there is any further information which I/we
can supply, please feel free to write me/us again.

Sincerely,

INTEROFFICE LETTERS AND MEMOS

(1) Announcement of Meeting

To: _____:

There will be a (name) meeting at the Hotel
(name) starting at (time, day, date), and running
through (day, date, time).

A complete agenda will be mailed to you shortly, but meantime you may want to make the necessary
arrangements. If you wish to stay/dine/lunch at the
Hotel (name), notify my secretary at once, and she
will make the reservation.

All salesmen/executives/secretaries/personnel
are expected to attend, and I would appreciate receiving immediate notice if, for some reason, you
are unable to be there

Cordially,

(2) Announcement of New Policies or Rules

To: _____:

    <u>Last</u>/<u>This week</u>/<u>month</u>/<u>year</u> a new policy <u>was</u>/<u>has been</u> adopted by (name of company) concerning (sub-ject).

    In order to simplify this procedure, all you need do is:

    (1) _____
    (2) _____
    (3) _____

    Please make sure you understand and follow <u>this rule</u>/<u>these rules</u>. <u>I</u>/<u>We</u> know <u>I</u>/<u>we</u> can count on the cooperation of each of you in this connection.

    Everyone benefits from a smoothly run organi-zation, so let's do our best to make the new policy work.

Cordially,

(3) Suggestions, Acknowledging

    a. Negative

Dear _____:

    Your suggestion concerning (subject of sugges-tion) has been thoroughly explored, and <u>I</u>/<u>we</u> wish to thank you for it.

    <u>Investigation indicates that it would not be practical to use your idea at this time because (reason). I/We have placed your suggestion on file in the event that, at some future time, I/we may find it worthy of reconsideration.</u>

    Meanwhile, many thanks for your participation.

Sincerely,

    b. Positive

    <u>Your idea is about to be put into practice, and we wish to assure you that you have made a valuable contribution to the company. A copy of this letter</u>

and your suggestion will become a part of your personnel record.

(4) Suggestions Requesting

To: _____

   We always welcome any suggestions from our employees to reduce costs, upgrade quality, or improve
procedures.
   Just drop your suggestion in the nearest box/
give your suggestion to your superior. Your idea
will receive prompt acknowledgment and, if quali-
fied, acceptance and appropriate recognition.
   Please be assured that whether or not your idea
is found acceptable, your participation is appreciated.

Cordially,

INTERVIEWS, JOB

(1) Granting to Someone

   a. Directly

Dear _____:

   The resume you sent me/us recently certainly
seems to indicate that you have the necessary background for a job as (job) here at (name of company).
   There may be an opening in the (name) department in about (time), so I'd suggest you come in to
see me on (day, date, time). At that time we can
discuss your qualifications for a position with us.
   If that date is not convenient, will you kindly
get in touch with me/us immediately?

Sincerely,

   b. Through Personnel

   Will you please come in for an interview with
our personnel manager, (name), on (day, date, time)?
After you talk with (name), I will be glad to see
you and discuss your qualifications for a position
with us.

c. Through Secretary

(Exec's name) has asked me to write to tell you
that (s)he will be happy to talk with you about your
qualifications for a position with us. (S)He will be
free to see you on (day, date, time).

(2) Refusing Someone

a. Applicant not Qualified

Dear _____ :

Thank you very much for your letter of (date),
in regard to the position of (name of job) with
(name of company).
Much as I would like to ask you to come in for
an interview, your resume indicates you are not
quite prepared to handle responsibilities which re-
quire some years of experience in the field. My suggestion would be to acquire further background as an
assistant to a (name of job), perhaps in a smaller
company.
Later on, if you are still interested in (name
of company), you might come in and fill out one of
our application forms so that we may place it on
file for future reference.

Cordially,

b. Someone Else Got There First

Much as I would like to ask you to come in for
an interview, we already have another applicant
whose qualifications seem eminently suited for the
job. I still believe your background and ability are
right for such a position, but there is nothing I
can do at the moment.

(3) Requesting Interview

Dear _____ :

Is there a need in your firm at this time for a

(name of job) with (number) years experience in the (name) field?

I'm a (year) graduate in (subject) of (name) University/College/Prep School/High School/Business School. The (name) Company, where I have been employed, is moving its offices out of town/is eliminating certain jobs in the interests of economy/does not offer me sufficient opportunity for advancement. As a result, I am seeking employment elsewhere.

In my present/recent position, it has been my responsibility to (give details). My background should prove of interest to (name) Company, as you can judge from the enclosed resume.

I shall appreciate a personal interview at your convenience.

Sincerely,

INTRODUCTIONS, SUPPLYING

(1) Business Associate

To: _____

This letter will introduce (name), who represents the firm of (name), (address).

I/We have known (name) for the past (number) years, and can vouch for his/her character and personality. The organization (s)he represents is one of the most respected in the field here in (place).

Any courtesy you may extend to (name) as a representative of (name of firm), will be much appreciated.

Sincerely,

(2) Business Organization

Dear _____:

May we introduce to you the (name) Company? We/They are new in (place), though we/they have been operating in (place) for (number) years. This expansion on our/their part now makes it possible for us/

them to offer you our/their (description) services/
products locally.

Our/Their customers include the (names of com-
panies) all known to you, I am sure. Any one of our/
their customers will be happy to anwer your questions about the organization.

They/I will phone you shortly with the hope
that you can set aside a quarter of an hour to discuss the ways in which (name of company) can be of
assistance to you.

Cordially,

(3) Executives and Friends

a. Executive

Dear _____:

(Name), bearer of this letter, is someone I
think you should meet. (S)He was recently appointed
(name of position) for (name) Company in (name of
locality).

Since (name) is now located in/will soon be
visiting your area, it occurred to me that you might
enjoy knowing one another. We both understand how
busy you are, but hoped you might get together at
some convenient time.

I'm sure you'll find the experience rewarding.

Sincerely,

b. Friend

(Name), bearer of this letter, is someone I
think you should meet. We have been friends for
(number) years, and I am sure you and (s)he would
have a lot in common. (S)He is (name of job) with
the (name) Company.

(4) Job Applicant

Dear _____:

    This letter will introduce (name) as a possible candidate for the (name) job with your firm, which I understand is available.

    I have known (name) for the past (number) years, and can vouch for his/her character and personality. His/Her background with (name) Company has provided excellent training, which should make him/her a worthy applicant for the position.

    Any consideration you may extend to (name) will be much appreciated.

Sincerely,

(5) Salesman or Representative

Dear _____:

    The (name) Company takes pleasure in introducing our new representative in your area, (name). (S)He is an expert in our field and can help you with your (description) problems.

    (Name) has contributed a great deal in the positions (s)he has held over the past (number) years, and would like to do as much for you. After a brief talk with (name), I'm sure you'll appreciate his/her sincerity and helpfulness.

    You can expect a visit/call from (name) next (day of week, time of day). Should you wish to phone, (s)he can be reached at (telephone number).

Cordially,

Chapter O ORDERS

Contents

Orders

ORDERS

(1) Canceling

a. Deadline Passed

Dear _____:

    We regret that circumstances force us to cancel our order of (date), Number (number), for (product).
    The deadline for delivery of this material/supply/item is long past and we can no longer use it as we had planned.
    We feel sure that, as a business person, you will understand the necessity for this cancellation.

Sincerely,

b. Need Passed

    The order we had for (our product or service) has been canceled, so we no longer need (your product).

c. Plans Changed

    We have changed our plans, and the (product) we ordered from you no longer fits our requirements.

(2) Placing

a. Estimate

Dear _____:

    We are pleased to place our order for (product), <u>in accordance with your estimate of (date)</u>.

Will you kindly make every effort to ship this <u>material/supply/item</u> by (date), so that we can fulfill our commitments.

Thank you for your promptness and cooperation.

Cordially,

b. No Estimate

<u>We are pleased to place our order for (amount)</u> <u>(merchandise) in (size, color, other description)</u>.

Chapter P   PAYMENTS THROUGH PRESENTATIONS

Contents

Payments Due

(see also C Collections)
Complaint About (see C Complaints)
Confirmation of Amount and Method
Misunderstanding by Others
Misunderstanding by You

Persuaders, Sales

Additional Information Offered
Quantity Offers Made
Reorders or Renewals Suggested
Time Limits Set

Presentations to Clients

Advertising Copy and Layouts
Reports on Studies and Surveys
Sales Promotion (see S Sales, Sales Promotion)

PAYMENTS DUE

(1) Confirmation of Amount and Method

Dear _____ :

This will confirm our mutual agreement to <u>start</u> <u>work on (job)</u>/<u>supply you with (material or service)</u> as soon as possible. The <u>work</u>/<u>material</u>/<u>service</u> will conform to specifications as approved by you as of (date).

For your records, the cost of <u>work</u>/<u>material</u>/ <u>service</u> will be (amount), to be paid (amount) percent now. Another (amount) percent will be due (time). The balance is payable (time).

Thank you for this opportunity to serve you.

Cordially,

(2) Misunderstanding by Others

Dear _____ :

<u>Today</u>/<u>Yesterday</u>/<u>This week</u>/<u>Last week</u> <u>I</u>/<u>we</u> received your invoice (number), dated (date), in the amount of (amount).

It was <u>my</u>/<u>our</u> understanding that the <u>material</u>/ <u>product</u>/<u>service</u> we bought from you would be billed <u>at a (number) percent discount</u>/<u>in monthly install-</u> <u>ments</u>. Will you please ask your <u>billing</u>/<u>credit de-</u> <u>partment</u> to cancel this invoice and issue a new one in the correct amount?

Thank you.

Sincerely,

(3) Misunderstanding by You

Dear _____:

You were perfectly right to return our invoice (number), dated (date), in the amount of (amount).

Our billing/credit department misunderstood the terms under which you made your purchase, but they now indicate they will be more than happy to co-operate.

Consequently, you will be billed at a (number) percent discount/in monthly installments in accordance with your request.

Please excuse the error. We appreciate your calling it to our attention.

Sincerely,

PERSUADERS, SALES

(1) Additional Information Offered

Dear _____:

Since our last meeting, (name), I have given a great deal of thought to some of the questions you raised. As a result, I have secured information which I believe will provide you with satisfactory answers.

If you will just tell your secretary when I may present you with this material, I'll call your office in a few days and arrange to drop by.

Cordially,

(2) Quantity Offers Made

Dear _____:

Everyone these days is looking for ways to beat inflation. One of the most effective methods is to order in volume whenever possible to take advantage of quantity discounts.

Our records show that during (year), you purchased (number) (description) (product), and (number) (description) (product). Since you never ordered more than (number) of these at a single time, you bought at a higher price than necessary, since discounts apply only on purchases of (number) at a time.

In amounts of (number) for each order, you could have cut your total costs for the year by (amount). That would have meant (amount) in additional <u>savings/profits</u> for you. And if you had ordered in (number) quantities, you could have <u>saved/cleared</u> another (amount).

We are always ready to cooperate with customers like you, whose credit is good, so why not discuss it with one of our representatives?

<u>I/We</u> hope to hear from you soon.

Cordially,

(3) Reorders or Renewals Suggested

Dear _____:

We thought you'd like to be reminded that the time is getting close when you will want to <u>place your next order for/renew your subscription to</u> (publication, book club, material, product, or service).

You have probably been meaning to <u>reorder/renew</u>, but just haven't got around to it. Too busy with other things, no doubt. To make sure you <u>don't run short/don't overlook it/miss no issues/miss no books</u>, won't you fill out and return the enclosed order form now?

If you have already <u>reordered/renewed</u>, please disregard this reminder.

Sincerely,

(4) Time Limits Set

Dear _____:

Some time ago, when we discussed the subject,

I thought you were seriously interested in purchasing (amount or description) (product, products, material, space, property).

Now I find that it will be necessary to close the deal quickly <u>before the price goes up</u>/<u>because I have someone else interested</u>.

Since time is limited, I would suggest that you get in touch with me by (day, date). I am sure the (product, products, material, space, property) would be ideal for the purpose you have in mind.

I'll be waiting to hear from you, (name).

Cordially,

PRESENTATIONS TO CLIENTS

(1) Advertising Copy and Layouts

Dear _____:

With this letter I'm sending the (number) <u>layouts</u>/<u>pieces of copy</u> for your (description) advertising campaign.

We think our <u>art</u>/<u>copy</u> department has done an excellent job in coming up with something that will really put your message across.

I hope you will agree, (name).

Cordially,

(2) Reports on Studies and Surveys

Dear _____:

In accordance with your instructions, <u>I</u>/<u>we</u> have made a survey to determine the advisability of (description of proposed action). The results of <u>my</u>/<u>our</u> investigation, along with <u>my</u>/<u>our</u> <u>conclusions</u>/<u>recommendations</u> are included in the accompanying report.

In addition to the careful study given to (subject), this report has also attempted to present the thinking of other people who have considered similar <u>plans</u>/<u>projects</u>.

Included is a bibliography of our various

sources of information, including (name) of the (department or company or organization), and (name) of the (department or company or organization), who were unusually helpful.

Respectfully submitted,

Chapter R   REFUSALS
OR REGRETS,
REQUESTS
AND REPLIES

Contents

REFUSALS OR REGRETS

(1) Financial Backing or Contribution

a. Backing

Dear _____:

Thank you for your recent letter concerning
(subject).

<u>After careful consideration, we find that we
are unable to invest in your project at this time.
This is in no way to be interpreted as a lack of
confidence in its potential. However, an investment
of that size does not fit in with our current
budget.</u>

I'm sorry that we cannot assist you in your
objectives, although we wish you the greatest
success.

Cordially,

b. Contribution

<u>You will understand, I'm sure, that a company
like ours cannot support every worthwhile cause,
much as we would like to do so. Since we have already contributed to the (name) and (name), we regret that we must decline any further requests of
this nature.</u>

(2) Honor Declined

Dear _____ :

    Although I appreciate your offer of an <u>award</u>/
<u>medal</u>/<u>plaque</u>/<u>prize</u> for my work <u>in</u>/<u>on</u>/<u>about</u> (sub-
ject), I feel that there are others more justly en-
titled to this honor.

    While I cannot accept the <u>award</u>/<u>medal</u>/<u>plaque</u>/
<u>prize</u>, I do want you to know how pleased I am that
my work has come to your favorable attention.

    Thank you so much for your kindness.

Sincerely,

REQUESTS AND REPLIES

(1) Assistance Offered for a Function

Dear _____ :

    I would very much like to <u>attend</u>/<u>take part in</u>/
<u>join</u>/<u>assist with</u> your <u>fund</u>/<u>bazaar</u>/<u>group</u> at (place)
in (location) on (date).

    As you know, <u>I</u>/<u>we</u> <u>am</u>/<u>are</u> in a position to make
a contribution in the area of <u>publicity</u>/<u>equipment</u>/
<u>ticket sales</u>. If you need help in this regard,
please call on <u>me</u>/<u>us</u>.

    Don't hesitate to let <u>me</u>/<u>us</u> know how <u>I</u>/<u>we</u> can
be of help in the wonderful work you are doing.

Sincerely,

(2) Cooperation Requested for a Function

Dear _____ :

    We would very much like to have you <u>attend</u>/<u>take
part in</u>/<u>join</u>/<u>assist with</u> our <u>fund</u>/<u>bazaar</u>/<u>group</u> at
(place) in (location) on (date).

    If you are in a position to make a contribution

in the area of <u>publicity</u>/<u>equipment</u>/<u>ticket sales</u>, we would be grateful for your help in this regard.

Any assistance you can offer us will be appreciated, and your presence will be more than welcome.

Cordially,

(3) Services Required for New Offices

Dear _____:

We plan to move to the (number) floor of the (name) Building on (name or number <u>street</u>/<u>avenue</u>/<u>square</u>/<u>plaza</u>/<u>place</u>, on (date), and we shall appreciate anything you can do to expedite <u>telephone</u>/<u>electric</u>/<u>cleaning</u>/<u>(other)</u> service by that time.

We shall need (description of service requirements). I would appreciate it greatly if you will make the necessary arrangements as soon as possible. Our credit references are (name) and (name).

Sincerely,

(4) Services Tendered for New Offices

Dear _____:

Thank you for your letter of the (date) about providing you with (description) service for your new offices.

We will send our (title), (name), along with a service man, to the (number) floor on (day, time) to go over the requirements. If this date is not convenient, please call <u>me</u>/<u>us</u> immediately, and <u>I</u>/<u>we</u> will be glad to make other arrangements.

Sincerely,

Chapter S   SALES, SALES PROMOTION THROUGH SOCIAL

Contents

SALES, SALES PROMOTION

(1) Advertising Solicitation

Dear _____:

   The (date) issue of (name of publication) is
one we feel sure will be of interest to you.
   In that issue (number) illustrated feature ar-
ticle(s) will be devoted to the subject of (subject). Don't you agree that this would be an excellent time to let our (number) readers know about
your (description) products?
   The closing date for our (date) issue is
(date). The sooner we hear from you, the choicer the
space we will be able to allocate to you.

Cordially,

(2) Before a Call

Dear _____:

   No doubt you have been hearing about the (name
of product). Now you can see it and try it yourself
right in your own office. Once you have seen its
many advantages, such as:

   1)
   2)
   3)

you'll wonder how you ever got along without it.
   Just drop the enclosed stamped, self-addressed
card in the mail to let me know when it would be

convenient for me to give you a demonstration. For
quicker action you can phone me at (number).

Cordially,

(3) Between Calls

a. Samples of New Line

Dear _____:

Although my next scheduled visit to you is
(time), I have a particular reason for getting in
touch with you ahead of time.

I am sending you some samples of our new line
of (product),I'd like you to see, so you won't be
delayed in obtaining whatever supplies you want.
Since we expect these items to be in great demand,
I'd suggest you place your order as soon as possible if you are interested.

I'll see you at/in/on (date or time) in any
case, and meantime warmest good wishes.

Cordially,

b. Spot Check of Inventory

Since business has been unusually active this
season, I'd suggest you make an inventory check in
case you need some replacements before I get there.
I'll phone you (time, date) to take care of your
needs, if any.

(4) Customer Unavailable

a. Appointment Broken

Dear _____:

I was sorry to learn that you could not keep
our appointment for (date) to discuss (subject), but
I understand you were unable to leave a meeting/your
schedule was unexpectedly changed/something came up
that prevented your being there/you were not feeling well.

When you have a <u>free moment/are feeling better</u>
won't you please call me so we can arrange <u>an/anoth-</u>
<u>er</u> appointment? I am anxious to be of service to
you, and feel sure I can assist you with your (subject) <u>program/problems/plans</u>. If I do not hear from
you by (time), I'll assume you'd prefer me to call
you.

Sincerely,

b. Casual Call

<u>Sorry I missed you when I dropped in (day of</u>
<u>week). You are, no doubt, familiar with our (name of</u>
<u>product, medium, or service), and I would like to</u>
<u>discuss its advantages for your particular needs</u>.

(5) Following a Call or Presentation

Dear _____:

Many thanks for giving me the opportunity to
discuss with you the subject of (subject) on (day
or date). It was a pleasure meeting with you, and I
look forward to a further exchange of ideas.

I'll phone you on (day) for another appointment, when <u>you have had a chance to think things</u>
<u>over/I have gathered some more material I think</u>
<u>you'll find of interest</u>.

Sincerely,

(6) Following a Sale

Dear _____:

I am most grateful for the business you gave me
(day or date). Your confidence means a great deal
to me, and I shall do my best to see that your <u>order</u>
<u>is filled/program is carried out/requirements are</u>
<u>taken care of</u> promptly and accurately.

You'll be hearing from me from time to time to
make sure that things are going well, and I'll be
happy to have you call me whenever I can be of further assistance.
My sincere thanks.

Cordially,

(7) Following a Turn-Down

Dear _____:

Although our meeting (day) resulted in no definite sale, I sincerely appreciate your giving me so
much of your valuable time.
Perhaps, at some future date, <u>I can come up
with suggestions that will fit your needs/we can
work something out together</u>.
Meanwhile, thanks for your pleasant reception.

Cordially,

(8) Follow-up of Undecided

Dear _____:

During the (days, week, weeks, month, months)
that <u>has/have</u> passed since I had the pleasure of
meeting with you, I hope you have had time to come
to a decision regarding (subject).
There are a number of advantages to the (product, service, facilities) we have to offer, the
main elements of which are:

    1)
    2)
    3)

I'll phone you <u>in a day or two/later in the
week/next week</u>, and perhaps we can get together to
bring our transaction to a happy conclusion for
both of us.

Cordially,

(9) Mail Order Catalog

Dear _____:

If your shopping time is limited, why not use the (name) Catalog, and save hours of pushing through crowds and waiting to be served.

The (name) Company for (number) years has been mailing its/the enclosed catalog without charge to grateful shoppers. This year's issue, with (number) pages, offers prospective customers a total of (number) items of clothing/housewares/stationery/hardware/novelties/toys/(other). Sizes and prices are indicated, and many/most/all are illustrated for your purchasing guidance.

The (name) policy of quality merchandise at moderate prices means that you can do your shopping economically without leaving your home. We'd like to have you join the (name) family, so do fill in and mail the enclosed postage-paid postcard/convenient order blank, and our catalog/your merchandise will be sent to you promptly.

Cordially,

(10) Referrals Requested

Dear _____:

Your recent expression of praise for our (product, service or facility, was a source of great pleasure to me.

Since you have found our (product, service, or facility) so satisfactory, it has occurred to me that you might be willing to do me the great favor of giving me the names and addresses of two or three friends or associates who might also benefit from the use of our (product, service, facility).

I'll give you a call when you may have had a chance to come up with some suitable prospects.

Cordially,

SEASONAL WISHES

(1) Chanukah, Christmas, New Year, Easter, Passover

Dear _____:

    As <u>Chanukah</u>/<u>Christmas</u>/<u>the New Year</u>/<u>Easter</u>/<u>Pass-</u><u>over</u> approaches, <u>I am</u>/<u>we are</u> happy in the knowledge that <u>I</u>/<u>we</u> can count you among <u>my</u>/<u>our</u> <u>clients</u>/<u>cus-</u><u>tomers</u>/<u>associates</u>.

    <u>I</u>/<u>We</u> consider this an appropriate time to express <u>my</u>/<u>our</u> appreciation for your <u>patronage</u>/<u>coop-</u><u>eration</u>/<u>confidence</u>, and to extend <u>my</u>/<u>our</u> best wishes for you and yours for the coming holiday.

Cordially,

SOCIAL LETTERS

(1) Accompanying Gifts

Dear _____:

    I'm sending along this little package in the hope that it is something which will help make your <u>birthday</u>/<u>holiday</u>/<u>anniversary</u> a happy one.

    With best wishes, (name), for a joyous <u>birth-</u><u>day</u>/<u>holiday</u>/<u>anniversary</u>.

Cordially,

(2) Anniversary

Dear _____:

    Allow me to congratulate you and (name of spouse) on your (number) wedding anniversary.

    Please accept my best wishes for your continued happiness and well-being.

Cordially,

(3) Birth

Dear _____:

    I was so pleased to receive the announcement of
the birth of (name). Becoming a parent is one of the
greatest experiences in the world. I know how proud
you and (name of spouse) must be of your little
girl/boy.
    My sincere congratulations to you both.

Cordially,

(4) Birthday

Dear _____:

    An informer, who shall remain nameless, has re-
minded me of the fact that you will celebrate your
birthday on (day).
    My informant did not reveal which birthday you
will be celebrating, but I do hope it will be an ex-
ceptionally happy one.
    Wishing you a delightful day and many, many
more.

Cordially,

(5) Congratulations

Dear _____:

    I was delighted to learn of your achievement in
the field of (subject).
    It will be a source of great pleasure to me in
years to come to be able to say, ''I knew him/her
when--.''
    No one deserves such recognition of his/her
abilities more than you.

Sincerely,

(6) Sympathy

a. Business Associate's Widow(er)

Dear _____:

I would like to express my sorrow at the recent death of your <u>husband/wife/(title of official)</u>.

In the <u>short/long</u> time it was my privilege to enjoy (name's) friendship, I found <u>him/her</u> a sincere and helpful associate, with whom it was a pleasure to <u>work/do business</u>.

<u>The knowledge that my thoughts are with you at this time will</u>, I hope, <u>be of some comfort to you</u>.

Sincerely,

b. Death of Company Executive

<u>I know what a serious loss this will be to everyone at (name of company). Please accept my sympathy</u>.

(7) Wedding

Dear _____:

May I offer my sincerest <u>congratulations/best wishes</u> to you on your <u>coming/recent</u> marriage?

Here's to much happiness and joy for both of you, now and in the years to come.

Cordially,

Chapter T   THANK YOU'S

Contents

Thank You's

THANK YOU'S

(1) Advice Appreciated

Dear _____:

   It is just (length of time) since I consulted
with you about (subject), and I want to assure you
that I appreciate your help.
   Your advice has been invaluable, and I have
followed the course you recommended, with gratifying results. I took the job/turned down the job/ap-
plied for the job/signed the contract/invested the
money/made the change/(other), and consider it the
wisest step I could have taken.
   I would like to express my gratitude, along
with my very best wishes.

Cordially,

(2) Gift Received

Dear _____:

   When you left a package for me yesterday/a few
days ago/last week, I had difficulty waiting until
my birthday/my anniversary/the holiday to open it.
   I don't know how to thank you, (name), for such
an attractive present. It is something that will
give me pleasure for a long time to come.
   Please accept my sincere thanks and best/holi-
day wishes.

Cordially,

(3) Hospitality Enjoyed

    a. Without Gift

Dear _____ :

    Thank you for a delightful stay.

    Your home is lovely, your meals delectable, and
<u>I/we</u> enjoyed the fun and companionship. <u>I am/We are</u>
still thinking about it and enjoying it in retro-
spect.

    Many thanks again for your warm hospitality.

Cordially,

    b. With Gift

    <u>I/We would like to express my/our thanks for
your warm hospitality with a little present that
you will shortly receive</u>.

(4) Luncheon or Dinner

Dear _____ :

    Thank you so much for the <u>luncheon/dinner</u> on
(day of week). I enjoyed being with <u>you/you and
(name or names)/the group</u> very much. The food was
good, but the company was what really mattered.

    Please accept my appreciation for the oppor-
tunity to chat with <u>you/both of you/all of you</u>. I
hope to repeat the pleasure in the near future.

Cordially,

(5) Salary Increase or Bonus

Dear _____ :

    Thank you very much for the recent <u>salary in-
crease/bonus</u>.

    A financial reward is always gratifying, be-
cause it assures an employee that his efforts are
appreciated. This <u>bonus/increase</u> could not have come

along at a better time since <u>I am planning to get married</u>/(name) and I are expecting a baby/<u>we are moving to a new home</u>/(other), and <u>wedding gifts</u>/<u>Blue Cross</u>/<u>home loans</u>/(other) can't cover all our needs.

    Thanks again sincerely,

Cordially,

PART THREE

Appendix

(A) How to Create Your Own
   Instant Letters
(B) Letter Styles and Format
(C) Forms of Address

Appendix (A)   HOW TO CREATE YOUR OWN INSTANT LETTERS

Contents

Each office has a certain amount of routine correspondence that is applicable to its particular business or professional operation. In some such situations, which the instant letters in this book cannot always cover exactly, you may want to improvise your own additional personal file of form letters.

SETTING UP A SUPPLEMENTARY BOOK

(1) Select Your Typical Letters

Try to recall the kind of letter you find yourself writing most often. Pull a dozen or two such letters from the files. Divide them into subjects covered. Find the examples of each that could apply most generally.

Xerox these typical letters, after crossing out proper names and dates, and anything else that needs to be changed from letter to letter. If you prefer, you can type them up, with proper names and dates omitted, and an alternate choice of words where necessary.

(2) Prepare a Loose Leaf Cover

After you have set up a series of typical letters, get yourself a large loose-leaf cover that will hold letter-size pages. A six-ring book is preferable.

Provide two blank pages for indexing purposes. Then cut each succeeding page into three equal parts, top, middle, and bottom. The six-ring book will hold each section of these three-part pages most securely.

(3) Make an Index

Make an index on the first page, with the half dozen or so subject headings under which your average routine correspondence might be classified.

Subject Headings

A	Adjustments
B	Billing
C	Collections
F	Follow-ups
O	Orders
S	Sales Promotion

The subject heading abbreviations will be indicated on index tabs directing you to the part of the book you want.

Your letters will be divided into sections, consisting of first paragraph, middle paragraph or paragraphs, and closing paragraph. Each paragraph is indicated by an identifying number, so you would follow the above index with a detailed one, indicating in a single line the number, form, and thought of the paragraph. For example:

Orders

First paragraph

0 1 It is a pleasure. Order Packed. Date to be received.
0 2 We are pleased. Indicate sizes you want.
0 3 We appreciate order, but regret line discontinued.
0 4 We want to assure you supplementary order shipped.

Middle paragraphs

0 21 Since you are a new customer, etc.
0 22 We were going to ship, but what size?
0 23 The model you ordered has been replaced by. . .
0 24 We are sending a catalogue.

Closing paragraph

0 31 We wish you success. Representative will call.
0 32 We look forward to opportunity serving.
0 33 Thank you for cooperation.
0 34 Assuring you of our desire to serve.

(4) Use of Paragraph Index

If you wanted to give a customer information about shipment of his order, send him a copy of your catalogue, and end with a hope for future business, you would choose *0 1*, *0 24*, and *0 32*.

If you were in the men's hat business the result might be:

Gentlemen:

It is a pleasure to receive your order for 12 dozen men's dark gray felt hats. The order is now being packed for shipment. You should receive it well before September 1, the date you specified.

In another envelope we are sending you our spring catalogue of men's felt, straw, and cloth

hats. You will find it convenient for future reference.

　　We look forward to a further opportunity of
serving you.

Sincerely,

(5) Match Up Index Tabs and Paragraphs

　　After you have made up your paragraph index, then you need to make
up index tabs to match. Fasten first paragraph index tabs on each of the top
sections. Do the same with middle paragraph tabs on the middle sections, and
closing paragraph tabs on the bottom sections. Next, place each paragraph on
its appropriate page section, either by cutting and cementing it on, or by
typing it directly.

　　Now, because of its structure, you have only to turn the sections of the
pages to have before you any combination of first, middle, and closing
paragraphs. The index tabs would look like this:

A 1	B 1	C 1
A 2	B 2	C 2
A 3	B 2	C 3
A 4	B 4	C 4
A 21	B 21	C 21
A 22	B 22	C 22
A 23	B 23	C 23
A 24	B 24	C 24
A 31	B 31	C 31
A 32	B 32	C 32
A 33	B 33	C 33
A 34	B 34	C 34

and so on, down the line.

　　The person using this book will gradually become familiar with the
contents of the paragraphs and will be able to choose them from the index.
To use the letter book, it is only necessary to note the index tab numbers of
the paragraphs to be used in the reply, on the letter being answered. The
reply is then typed after turning to the paragraphs in the form book.

(6) Final Setup

　　The final setup for a typical letter would look something like the
following:

0 1   0 1

It is a pleasure to receive your order for _____
_____. The order is now being packed for ship-
ment. You should receive it well before _____,
the date you specified.

0 24   0 24

In another envelope we are sending you our _____
catalogue of _____. You will find it convenient for future reference.

0 32   0 32

We look forward to a further opportunity of serving
you.

With more explicit provision for the insertion of amounts, names, dates, and other information, the paragraphs would appear like this:

0 1   0 1

It is a pleasure to receive your order for (amount,
description, merchandise). The order is now being
packed for shipment. You should receive it well before (date), the date you specified.

0 24   0 24

In another envelope we are sending you our (name)
catalogue of (description, merchandise). You will
find it convenient for future reference.

(7) Practical Uses

Though the amount of written words in the book may equal only as few as 25 three-paragraph letters, due to its mechanical construction, the book can be manipulated so that hundreds of different letters could be written with the 75 paragraphs contained therein. Because of the way the form paragraphs are collated, it is possible to write letters whose contents embody paragraphs on as many different subjects as necessary.

The order letter about men's hats could, for example, also use a paragraph about adjustments of previous orders, *A 22*, or collection of a previous bill, *C 23*. Then the letter would read like either of these:

Gentlemen:

It is a pleasure to receive your order for 12 dozen men's dark gray felt hats. The order is now being packed for shipment. You should receive it well before September 1, the date you specified.

We are very sorry you found several hats in the previous shipment unsatisfactory. If you will return them, we will make the adjustment you request.

In another envelope we are sending you our spring catalogue of men's felt, straw, and cloth hats. You will find it convenient for future reference.

We look forward to further opportunities of serving you.

Sincerely,

Gentlemen:

It is a pleasure to receive your order for 12 dozen men's dark gray felt hats. The order is now being packed for shipment. You should receive it well before September 1, the date you specified.

In looking over your account, we note there still remains a small balance of $200 now overdue for some time. We would appreciate your bringing the account up to date.

In another envelope we are sending you our spring catalogue of men's felt, straw, and cloth hats. You will find it convenient for future reference.

We look forward to a further opportunity of serving you.

Sincerely,

(8) Further Variations

This order letter can be changed further by omitting reference to the catalogue, or by leaving out the closing paragraph. The variations on any particular letter are limitless. You can close with "Season's Greetings," when it is that time of year. You can always insert a personal paragraph, or one that is specially written to suit the special situation. You can remove a paragraph from the book and replace it with another if, for some reason, it becomes outdated or overworked. The book can be expanded as time goes on to accommodate more and more of your routine correspondence.

It is a good idea to use alternative opening and closing sentences for similar letters written frequently to the same people.

For instance, *It is a pleasure to receive your order* should be alternated with *We appreciate your order, We are pleased to have your order, We are happy to acknowledge your order*, or any other variation that occurs to you.

Similarly, *We look forward to a further opportunity to serve you*, can be alternated with *Assuring you of our desire to serve you, We wish you success in the coming season*, or *We are always glad to be of service*.

Another way to vary your form letters is by personalizing them. Our sample letter could be made to sound more personal with the addition of the following underlined words:

Dear Mr. Wisdom:

It is a pleasure to receive your order for 12 dozen men's dark gray felt hats. The order is now being packed for shipment, <u>Mr. Wisdom</u>. You should receive it in <u>Kansas City</u> well before September 1, the date you specified.

In another envelope we are sending you our spring catalogue of men's felt, straw, and cloth hats. You <u>and your associates at Young and Company</u> will find it convenient for future reference.

<u>As usual</u>, we look forward to a further opportunity to serve you.

Sincerely,

If this thought appeals to you, you might leave appropriate blanks in your form paragraphs where personalized references—though not essential—may be inserted effectively.

While it may take a little effort to set up this loose-leaf instant letter book, you'll find it worth the trouble in saved time and labor as you run your eye down the tabs on the right and pick out at a glance the paragraphs you need, one to start, one to close, and any number for in between.

Appendix (B) LETTER STYLES AND FORMAT

Contents

Openings and Closings

Address
Attention Line
Close
Salutation
Signature
Subject Line

Specific Styles

Block
Block (Full)
Indented
Official
Semiblock
Simplified

OPENINGS AND CLOSINGS

(1) Address

a. Abbreviations

The inside address on a letter should correspond with the official name of the company being addressed. Follow the form they, themselves, use, whether it be *Company*, *Co.*, *Limited*, *Ltd.*, *The*, *Inc.*, or whatever.

The numbered street in the address should never be followed with a *th*, *st*, *nd*, or *rd*. Words that stand for street direction, South, North, West, East, should be abbreviated only when you feel it necessary to keep a long line short. Also, spell out the numerical names of streets and avenues that are numbered 12 or under. The names of cities or towns are rarely abbreviated.

Names of states, territories and U.S. possessions may be abbreviated when zip codes are used. The zip code follows the state and is not separated from it by a comma.

Do not abbreviate titles of positions, such as *President*, *Treasurer*, *Secretary*, *General Manager*. The usual *Mr.*, *Mrs.*, or *Miss* precedes an individual's name, even when the business title is used.

Mr. Abraham A. Acheson, President
Acheson & Beame Company
123 Park Avenue South
New York, NY 10016

Mrs. Caroline C. Cardwell, Vice President
The Davidson Company, Ltd.
456 East Tenth Street
Chicago, IL 60411

b. Placement

The address should begin not less than two spaces nor more than twelve, below the date line. Although it can be placed at the foot of the letter, flush with the left margin, the standard form is at the top. In the block layout, the end of a long line may be carried over to a second line, indented three spaces.

> The Institute of Electrical
>   and Electronics Engineers
> 345 East 47 Street

(2) Attention Line

The attention line is used to indicate that the letter may be opened by someone else than the person to whom it is directed, if necessary. It is also used as a way out when you don't know the initials of the man or woman to whom you are writing. It is typed two spaces below the address and is not underlined.

> Feldman Corporation
> 188 Maple Street
> Springfield, MA 01125
> Attention: Miss Grace G. Giles
> Gentlemen:

OR:

> Feldman Corporation
> 188 Maple Street
> Springfield, MA 01125
>
>   Attention, Miss Grace G. Giles
> Gentlemen:

Such a letter is always addressed to the organization, and never to the individual, in the salutation, as you will have noted.

(3) Close

a. Placement

The complimentary close is typed two spaces beneath the last line of the letter. Start it a bit to the right of center, except in the full block and simplified letter styles. Never allow the complimentary close to extend beyond the right margin of the letter.

b. Punctuation

Capitalize the first word of the close only. Follow the close with a comma.

c. Styles

The trend today is toward informality, so that we rarely use the old-fashioned "Very truly yours," or "Respectfully yours," and their variations, unless in a very formal letter in which the person is addressed as "Sir" or "Madam."

The usual signature is a simple, "Sincerely," or the slightly warmer, "Cordially."

(4) Salutation

a. Placement

The salutation is typed two spaces below the inside address, flush with the left-hand margin. If an attention line is used, the salutation is placed two lines below.

b. Punctuation

Capitalize the first word, the title, and the name in the salutation. Follow the salutation with a colon.

My dear Mrs. Hartford:
Dear Mr. Ichabod:

c. Titles

Mr., *Mrs.* and *Dr.* are the only titles that are abbreviated, and *Doctor* is preferable to *Dr.*

A title is never used following a salutation, and it is never used without a surname. A business title is never used in a salutation.

Dear *Dr./Mr./Doctor* Manville: (Not Dear Mr. Manville, Ph.D.:)
Dear Professor Jones: (Not Dear Professor:)
Dear Mr. King: (Not Dear President King:)

When no particular individual is addressed, then a plural salutation is used.

Gentlemen: Ladies: Mesdames: Ladies and Gentlemen:

A man and woman are addressed jointly as *Dear Sir and Madam*, or *Dear Mr.* (Name) and *Miss/Mrs.* (Name). A married couple are, of course, addressed as *Dear Mr. and Mrs.* (Name).

(5) Signature and Initials

a. Placement

The modern practice is to omit the firm name in the signature of a letter, except when it is a formal document. The name of the writer is typed at the bottom of a letter, four spaces beneath the complimentary close. His business title is typed beneath his name, unless the letter is a personal one. If the firm name is included, it is typed two spaces below the close, with the writer's name four spaces below the firm name. No part of the signature should extend beyond the right-hand margin of the letter.

b. Secretary's Initials and Signature

If your organization uses the initial identification line, type the initials of dictator and stenographer flush with the left-hand margin, one space below the last line of the close.

When you sign an executive's name to a letter, your initials should be written right below it. If you sign the letter in your own name, as your employer's secretary, precede his or her name by *Mr.*, *Dr.*, *Mrs.*, or *Miss*, and omit the initials unless another person in the firm has the same name.

Secretary to Mr. Nolan (Not Secretary to N. N. Nolan
or Secretary to Mr. N. N. Nolan)

c. Women's Signatures

A woman's name should be signed in full, as her surname prece. .. .y initials can cause confusion as to her identity.

A divorcee should never use her ex-husband's given name. Her typed signature uses her own first name or her maiden name, combined with her husband's surname:

(Mrs.) Olive O. Osborn   or (Mrs. Owen Osborn)
(Not Mrs. Olive O. Osborn)

A married woman may precede her typed signature with (Mrs.), or she may have her married name typed in parentheses beneath her written signature. Some women in business allow themselves to be addressed as *Miss* and their signature is typed without indicating their married state, just as a man's would be.

(Mrs.) Paula Prentice   (Mrs. Paul Prentice)   Paula Prentice

A single woman may precede her typed signature with (Miss), but this is not customary. A widow signs her name in the same way as any other married woman.

(6) Subject Line

a. Placement

The subject line follows the salutation, two spaces below it. In full block or simplified letter style, the subject line is placed flush with the left-hand margin. Otherwise, it is centered.

The subject line is never placed before the salutation, as it is part of the body of the letter.

b. Punctuation

All important words in a subject line are capitalized. Sometimes the word *Subject* is used to introduce the line. It is usually underlined and followed by a colon. However, the modern method is to omit the introductory word and underscore the line itself.

In legal letters the subject is usually preceded by the expression *In Re*, with no following colon.

Parker Publishing Company, Inc.
West Nyack, NY 10994

Gentlemen:

Fall Publication List

SPECIFIC STYLES

(1) Block

In block style letters, the inside address and paragraphs are blocked flush with the left margin, and the salutation and attention line, if any, aligned with the inside address. However, date and reference lines are flush with the right margin, and the typed signature and close are also at the right. Open punctuation is used.

September 16, 19XX

Miss Ruth Roland
Consolidated Chemical Trust Co.
222 Sixth Avenue
New York, NY 10003

Dear Miss Roland:

It is that time of year again when we appeal to you as a loyal friend of the League of Women Voters to continue your valued support.
The New York City League is called upon to:

1) Provide answers to the thousands of citizens who call their Telephone Information Service.
2) Set up registration and voting information projects for banks, businesses, and civic groups.

3) Meet public demand for best-sellers like FACTS
FOR VOTERS and THEY REPRESENT YOU.
4) Fill the TV and radio airwaves with League's nonpartisan election information.

<u>And we can do more</u>! It's up to generous people like
you, who want to make a contribution to their community through the League of Women Voters. We sincerely appreciate your past gifts, and hope you will
again invest in good government.
Please send your check today!

                        Sincerely,

                        Jean C. Vermes

JCV:jp

(2) Block (Full)

In full block style all structural parts begin flush with the left margin,
and there are no indentations. Open punctuation is used in the address and
signature, and the dictator's initials are not included in the identification line.

September 16, 19XX

Miss Ruth Roland
Consolidated Chemical Trust Co.
222 Sixth Avenue
New York, NY 10003

Dear Miss Roland:

It is that time of year again when we appeal to you
as a loyal friend of the League of Women Voters to
continue your valued support.
The New York City League is called upon to:

1) Provide answers to the thousands of citizens who
call their Telephone Information Service
2) Set up registration and voting information projects for banks, businesses, and civic groups.
3) Meet public demand for best-sellers like FACTS
FOR VOTERS and THEY REPRESENT YOU.

4) Fill the TV and radio airwaves with League's nonpartisan election information.
<u>And we can do more</u>! It's up to generous people like
you who want to make a contribution to their community through the League of Women Voters. We sincerely appreciate your past gifts, and hope you will
again invest in good government.
Please send your check today!

Sincerely,

Jean C. Vermes

jp

(3) Indented

    In indented style, each line of the address is indented five spaces more
than the preceding one, and the first line of each paragraph is indented ten
spaces. The typed signature is also indented three spaces from the beginning
of the complimentary close. Closed punctuation is used in the address.

                                        September 16, 19XX

Miss Ruth Roland,
        Consolidated Chemical Trust Co.,
            222 Sixth Avenue,
                New York, NY 10003

Dear Miss Roland:

            It is that time of year again when we ap-
peal to you as a loyal friend of the League of Women
Voters to continue your valued support.
            The New York City League is called upon
to:
        1)   Provide answers to the thousands of citi-
zens who call their Telephone Information Service.
        2)   Set up registration and voting information
projects for banks, businesses, and civic groups.

3)   Meet public demand for best-sellers like
FACTS FOR VOTERS and THEY REPRESENT YOU.
4)   Fill the TV and radio airwaves with
League's nonpartisan election information.
And we can do more! It's up to generous
people like you who want to make a contribution to
their community through the League of Women Voters.
We sincerely appreciate your past gifts, and hope
you will again invest in good government.
Please send your check today!

Sincerely,

Jean C. Vermes

(4) Official

The official style letter has the inside address placed below the signature, flush with the left-hand margin. Open punctuation is used, and the identification line and enclosure notations, if any, are typed two spaces below the last line of the address. This style is recommended for personal letters in business.

Dear Miss Roland:

It is that time of year again when we appeal to
you as a loyal friend of the League of Women Voters
to continue your valued support.
The New York City League is called up to:
1) Provide answers to the thousands of citizens
who call their Telephone Information Service.
2) Set up registration and voting information
projects for banks, businesses, and civic groups.
3) Meet public demand for best-sellers like
FACTS FOR VOTERS and THEY REPRESENT YOU.
4) Fill the TV and radio airwaves with League's
nonpartisan election information.
And we can do more! It's up to generous people
like you who want to make a contribution to their
community through the League of Women Voters. We

sincerely appreciate your past gifts, and hope you
will again invest in good government.
    Please send your check today!

                                        Sincerely,

                                        Jean C. Vermes

Miss Ruth Roland
Consolidated Chemical Trust Co.
222 sixth Avenue
New York, NY 10003

Enclosure

(5) Semiblock

    In the semiblock style, the structural parts of the letter are flush with
the left-hand margin, but the first line of each paragraph is indented five
spaces. The date is typed in the conventional position and the typed signature
and close are also at the right. Open punctuation is used.

                                        September 16, 19XX

Miss Ruth Roland
Consolidated Chemical Trust Co.
222 Sixth Avenue
New York, NY 10003

Dear Miss Roland:

    It is that time of year again when we appeal to
you as a loyal friend of the League of Women Voters
to continue your valued support.
    The New York City League is called upon to:
    1) Provide answers to the thousands of citizens
who call their Telephone Information Service.
    2) Set up registration and voting information
projects for banks, businesses, and civic groups.
    3) Meet public demand for best-sellers like
FACTS FOR VOTERS and THEY REPRESENT YOU.
    4) Fill the TV and radio airwaves with League's
nonpartisan election information.

And we can do more! It's up to generous people
like you who want to make a contribution to their
community through the League of Women Voters. We
sincerely appreciate your past gifts, and hope you
will again invest in good government.
      Please send your check today!

                              Sincerely,

                              Jean C. Vermes

(6) Simplified

In the simplified style, the salutation and complimentary close are
omitted. "Copy to" is also omitted before the names of persons to whom
carbons are to be sent. The letter is written completely flush with the
left-hand margin. The subject line is placed between the address and the body
of the letter. Open punctuation is used.

September 16, 19XX

Miss Ruth Roland
Consolidated Chemical Trust Co.
222 Sixth Avenue
New York, NY 10003

FINANCE DRIVE

It is that time of year again when we appeal to you
as a loyal friend of the League of Women Voters to
continue your valued support.
The New York City League is called upon to:

1) Provide answers to the thousands of citizens who
call their Telephone Information Service.
2) Set up registration and voting information projects for banks, businesses, and civic groups.
3) Meet public demand for best-sellers like FACTS
FOR VOTERS and THEY REPRESENT YOU.
4) Fill the TV and radio airwaves with League's nonpartisan election information.

And we can do more! It's up to generous people like
you who want to make a contribution to their com-

munity through the League of Women Voters. We sincerely appreciate your past gifts, and hope you will
again invest in good government.
Please send your check today!

JEAN C. VERMES

Appendix (C) FORMS OF ADDRESS

Contents

---

(1) Business Address

a. Company or Corporation

Albert Adams and Company,
(local address)
Gentlemen:

b. Corporation, Attention Individual

Batten, Barton and Company, Inc.
(local address)
Attention: Mr. Bradford Brown
Gentlemen:

c. Doctor

Dr. Cecil Chalmers   (*or* Cecil Chalmers, M.D.)
(local address)
Dear Dr. Chalmers:

d. Group of Men and Women

Art Students League of New York
(local address)
Ladies and Gentlemen:

e. Individual Man

Mr. David Downing
Daniel Doberman Company
(local address)
Dear Mr. Downing: (*or* Dear Sir:)

f. Lawyer

Mr. Everett E. Everest
Attorney at Law
(local address)
Dear Mr. Everest:

g. Two or More Men

Mr. Francis Farmer and
Mr. George Grant
(local address)
Dear Mr. Farmer and Mr. Grant: (*or* Gentlemen:)

h. Two or More Women

Mrs. Grace G. Glenville and
Miss Hildegarde Hampton
(local address)
Ladies: (*or* Dear Mesdames)

(2) Court Officials

a. Associate Justice, U.S. Supreme Court

Mr. Justice Alexander
The Supreme Court
Washington, D.C.
Sir: (*or* My dear Mr. Justice)

b. Chief Justice, State Supreme Court

The Honorable Bruce B. Brady
Chief Justice of the Supreme Court of (state)
(local address)
Sir: (*or* My dear Mr. Chief Justice:)
   (My dear Judge Brady:)

c. Chief Justice, U.S. Supreme Court

The Chief Justice
The Supreme Court
Washington, D.C.
Sir: (*or* My dear Mr. Chief Justice)

d. Clerks of Courts

Charles C. Conrad, Esquire
Clerk of the Superior Court
(local address)
Sir: (*or* My dear Mr. Conrad)

e. Judge of a Court

Judge of the United States District Court
   for the (location) District of (state)

(local address)
Sir: (*or* My dear Judge Dillon:)

f. Presiding Justice

The Honorable Edward E. Elgin
Presiding Justice, (description) Division
Supreme Court
(local address)
Sir: (*or* My dear Mr. Justice:)

g. Retired Justice, U.S. Supreme Court

The Honorable Frank F. Feldman
(local address)
Sir: (*or* Dear Justice Feldman)

(3) Educational Officials

a. Associate or Assistant Professor

Mr. Adam A. Astor or (doctor's degree) Adam A. Astor, Ph.D.
Associate (Assistant) Professor
Department of (name)
(local address)
Dear Sir: (Dear Professor Astor: *or* Dear Dr. Astor:)

b. Chaplain of College or University

The Reverend Barnard B. Baxter, D.D.
Chaplain, (name) College
(local address)
Dear Chaplain Baxter: (Dear Dr. Baxter)

c. Dean or Assistant Dean, College or Graduate School

Dean Clifford C. Canbury
    or (doctor's degree) Dr. Clifford C. Canbury, Dean (Assistant Dean)
(name of school)
(local address)
Dear Sir: (Dear Dean Canbury)

d. Dean, Female

Dean Dorothy D. Dover
    or (doctor's degree) Dr. Dorothy D. Dover, Dean (Assistant Dean)
(name of school)

(local address)
Dear Madam: (Dear Dean Dover)

e. Instructor, College or University

Mr. Elliot E. Evans
   or (doctor's degree) Elliot E. Evans, Ph.D.
(name of department)
(local address)
Dear Sir: (Dear Mr. Grant: Dear Dr. Grant:)

f. President, College or University

(doctor's degree)
Frank F. Forrester, L.L.D., Ph.D. *or* Dr. Frank F. Forrester
President, (name of school)
(local address)
Sir: (Dear Dr. Forrester)

(no doctor's degree)
Mr. Frank F. Forrester
President, (name of school)
(local address)
Sir: (Dear President Forrester)

(Catholic priest)
The Very Reverend Frank F. Forrester, S.J., D.D., Ph.D
President, (name of school)
(local address)
Sir: (Dear Father Forrester)

g. Professor

Professor George G. Grant
   (doctor's degree) George G. Grant, Ph.D.
(name of school)
(local address)
Dear Sir: (Dear Professor Grant)   (Dear Dr. Grant)

h. School Principal

(doctor's degree)
Dr. Henry H. Hewes or Henry H. Hewes, Ph.D.
Principal, (name of school)
(local address)

Dear Dr. Hewes:

(no doctor's degree)

Mr. Henry H. Hewes
Principal, (name of school)
(local address)

Dear Mr. Hewes:

i. University Chancellor

Dr. Irving I. Islip
Chancellor, (name of school)
(local address)

Dear Dr. Islip:

(4' Foreigh Officials

a. British Prime Minister

he Right Honorable Archibald A. Ambrose, K.G., M.C., M.P.
Prime Minister
London, England

Sir: (Dear Mr. Prime Minister: Dear Mr. Ambrose:)

b. Canadian Prime Miṇister

The Right Honorable Bernard B. Banville, C.M.G.
Prime Minister of Canada
Ottawa, Canada

Sir: (Dear Mr. Prime Minister: Dear Mr. Banville:)

c. Foreign Ambassador in United States

His Excellency, Charles C. Charbert
Ambassador of (country)
Washington, D.C.

Excellency: (Dear Mr. Ambassador:)

d. Foreign Charge d'Affaires in United States

Mr. David D. Davidson
Chargé d'Affaires of (country)
Washington, D.C.

Sir: (Dear Mr. Davidson)

e. Foreigh Chargé d'Affaires ad interim

Mr. Edward E. Edwards

Chargé d'Affaires ad interim of (country)
Washington, D.C.
Sir: (Dear Mr. Edwards)

f. Foreign Diplomatic Representative, Personal Title

His Excellency, (title) Frederick F. Fredericks
Ambassador of (country)
Washington, D.C.
Excellency: (Dear Mr. Ambassador)

g. Foreign Minister in the United States

The Honorable Gabriel G. Gabriels
Minister of (country)
Washington, D.C.
Sir: (Dear Mr. Minister)

h. Premier

His Excellency, Horace H. Horatio
Premier of the (country)
(local address)
Excellency: (Dear Mr. Premier:)

i. President of Republic

His Excellency, Ives I. Iverson
President of the Republic of (name)
(local address)
Excellency: (Dear Mr. President)

j. Prime Minister

His Excellency, John J. Johnson
Prime Minister of (country)
(local address)
Excellency: (Dear Mr. Prime Minister)

(5) Government Officials, State and Local

a. Acting Governor

The Honorable Albert A. Albertson
Acting Governor of (state)
(local address)
Sir: (Dear Mr. Albertson)

b. Alderman

Alderman Brian B. Brown
City Hall
(local address)
Dear Sir: (Dear Mr. Brown)

c. Attorney General

The Honorable Clifford C. Case
Attorney General of (state)
(local address)
Sir: (Dear Mr. Attorney General)

d. City Attorney, City Counsel, Corporation Counsel

The Honorable Dean D. Deacon, (title)
(local address)
Dear Sir: (Dear Mr. Deacon)

e. District Attorney

The Honorable Elliot E. Ellison
District Attorney, (name) County
County Courthouse
(local address)
Dear Sir: (Dear Mr. Ellison)

f. Governor of State

The Honorable the Governor of (state)
(local address)
Sir:

or

The Honorable Franklin F. Franks
Governor of (state)
(local address)
Dear Governor Franks:

g. Governor of State of Massachusetts

His Excellency, the Governor of Massachusetts
Boston, Massachusetts
Sir: (Dear Governor Franks)

h. Lieutenant Governor

The Honorable the Lieutenant Governor of (state)
(local address)
Sir:

or

The Honorable Grant G. Granville
Lieutenant Governor of (state)
(local address)
Dear Mr. Granville:

i. Mayor of a City

The Honorable Herbert H. Herrick
Mayor of (city)
(local address)
Dear Sir: (Dear Mayor Herrick)

j. President, Board of Commissioners

The Honorable Isaac I. Isaacson, President
Board of Commissioners of the City of (name)
(local address)
Dear Sir: (Dear Mr. Isaacson)

k. President, State Senate

The Honorable Jeremiah J. Josephs
President of the Senate of the State of (name)
(local address)
Sir: (Dear Mr. Josephs)

l. Secretary of State

The Honorable Secretary of State of (state)
(local address)
Sir:

or

The Honorable Kenneth K. Knowles
Secretary of State of (state)
(local address)
Dear Mr. Secretary:

m. Speaker of Assembly, House of Representatives

The Honorable Leonard L. Lyons
Speaker of the Assembly of the State of (name)
(local address)
Sir: (Dear Mr. Lyons)

n. State Representative, Assemblyman or Delegate

The Honorable Maxwell M. Maxville
House of Representatives
(local address)
Dear Sir: (Dear Mr. Maxville)

o. State Senator

The Honorable Norman N. Norcross
The State Senate
(local address)
Dear Sir: (Dear Mr. Norcross)

p. Treasurer, Auditor, or Comptroller

The Honorable Oscar O. Oswald
Treasurer of the State of (name)
(local address)
Dear Sir: (Dear Mr. Oswald)

(6) Government Officials, United States

a. American Ambassador

His Excellency, The American Ambassador
American Embassy (*or* Embassy of the United States
   of America)
(local address)
Dear Mr. Ambassador:

or

Her Excellency, The American Ambassador
American Embassy
(local address)
Dear Madam Ambassador:

b. Cabinet Officers, Secretary

The Honorable the Secretary of the (department)
Washington, D.C.

Sir: (Madam)

or

The Honorable Paul(a) P. Paulson
Secretary of the (Department)
Washington, D.C.
Dear Mr. Secretary: (Dear Madam Secretary)

c. Cabinet Officers, Special

(former cabinet officer)
The Honorable Quentin Q. Quinn
(local address)
Dear Sir: (Dear Mr. Quinn)

(Postmaster General)
The Honorable Roland R. Rogers
The Postmaster General
Washington, D.C.
Sir: (Dear Mr. Postmaster General)

(The Attorney General)
The Honorable Samuel S. Samson
The Attorney General
Washington, D.C.
Sir: (Dear Mr. Attorney General)

(Under Secretary)
The Honorable Thomas S. Thompson
Under Secretary of (department)
Washington, D.C.
Dear Mr. Thompson:

d. Congressmen, Committee Chairmen

(Committee)
The Honorable Ulysses U. Underwood, Chairman
Committee on (subject)
United States Senate
Washington, D.C.
Dear Mr. Chairman:

(Subcommittee)
The Honorable Vincent V. Vernon, Chairman
Subcommittee on (subject)

United States Senate
Washington, D.C.
Dear Senator Vernon:

e. Congressmen, Representatives

The Honorable W. W. Wylie
House of Representatives
Washington, D.C.
Dear Sir: (Dear Mr. Wylie)
Dear Madam: (Dear Mrs./Miss Wylie)

(at Large)
The Honorable Alan A. Atkins
House of Representatives
Washington, D.C.
Dear Mr. Atkins:

(former)
The Honorable Bradford B. Billings
(local address)
Dear Mr. Billings:

(resident commissioner)
        or delegate
The Honorable Carlo C. Carlos
Resident Commissioner of Puerto Rico (Delegate of Puerto Rico)
House of Representatives
Washington, D.C.
Dear Mr. Carlos:

f. Congressmen, Senators

The Honorable D. D. Desmond
United States Senate
Washington, D.C.
Dear Senator Desmond: .
Dear Mrs./Miss Desmond:

(-elect)
Honorable Edgar E. Edmond
Senator-elect
United States Senate
Washington, D.C.

Dear Mr. Edmond:

(*former*)

The Honorable Frederick F. Fontaine
(local address)

Dear Senator Fontaine:

(*Speaker of the House*)

The Honorable Speaker of the House of Representatives
Washington, D.C.

or

The Honorable Grant G. Gilbertson
Speaker of the House of Representatives
Washington, D.C.

Sir: (Dear Mr. Speaker or Dear Mr. Gilbertson)

(*Speaker, former*)

The Honorable Howard H. Herbert
(local address)

Sir: (Dear Mr. Herbert)

g. Consul

Irving I. Inglehart, Esq., American Consul
(local address)

Sir: (Dear Mr. Inglehart)

h. Executives, The President

The President
The White House
Washington, D.C.

Mr. President: (Dear Mr. President)

(*former*)

The Honorable Joseph J. Jackson
(local address)

Sir: (Dear Mr. Jackson)

(*Vice*)

The Vice President of the United States
United States Senate
Washington, D.C.

Sir: (Dear Mr. Vice President)

i. Heads or Directors of Independent Agencies

The Honorable Kurt K. King
Director, (name) Agency
Washington, D.C.
Dear Mr. *Director/Commissioner/Chairman*:
(Dear Mr. King)

j. Librarian of Congress

The Honorable Lawrence L. Lang
Librarian of Congress
Washington, D.C.
Dear Mr. Lang:

k. Minister Plenipotentiary

His Excellency, The American Minister
(local address)
or:
The Honorable M. M. Meredith
Legation of the United States of America
(local address)
Your Excellency: (Sir, Dear Mr. Minister, Dear Mr.
                  Meredith, Dear Madam Minister, or
                  Dear *Mrs./Miss* Meredith)

l. Secretaries to the President

The Honorable Nigel N. Norman
Secretary to the President
The White House
Washington, D.C.
Dear Mr. Norman:

(*Assistant*)
The Honorable Oliver O. Orwell
Assistant Secretary to the President
The White House
Washington, D.C.
Dear Mr. Orwell:

(*Military rank*)
(Title) Philip P. Patrick

Secretary to the President
The White House
Washington, D.C.
Dear (Title) Patrick:

(Press)

Mr. Randolph R. Rome
Press Secretary to the President
The White House
Washington, D.C.
Dear Mr. Rome:

m. U.S. Officials, Other

(Comptroller General)

The Honorable Sidney S. Samuels
Comptroller General of the United States
Washington, D.C.
Dear Mr. Samuels:

(Public Printer)

The Honorable Terence T. Tucker
Public Printer
Washington, D.C.
Dear Mr. Tucker:

(7) Military Personnel

a. Army Generals

General of the Army Arnold A. Aaron, U.S.A.
Department of the Army
Pentagon, Washington, D.C.
Sir: (Dear General Aaron)

General/*Brigadier* General/*Lieutenant* General/*Major* General
   Bernard B. Bishop, U.S.A.
(local address)
Sir: (Dear General Bishop)

b. Captain

Captain Claude C. Carol, U.S.A.
(local address)
Dear Captain Carol:

c. Chaplain

Chaplain Douglas D. Denver, Captain, U.S.A.
(local address)
Dear Chaplain Denver:

d. Colonel, Lieutenant Colonel

Colonel (Lieutenant Colonel) Egbert E. Elgin, U.S.A.
(local address)
Dear Colonel Elgin:

e. Lieutenant, First or Second

Lieutenant Foster F. Fairchild, U.S.A.
(local address)
Dear Lieutenant Fairchild:

f. Major

Major Gregory G. Gibbs, U.S.A.
(local address)
Dear Major Gibbs:

f-1. Marine Corps and Air Force address same as above, with initials U.S.M.C. and U.S.A.F. instead of U.S.A.

g. Navy Admirals

Fleet Admiral Horace H. Hines, U.S.N.
Chief of Naval Operations
Department of the Navy
Washington, D.C.
Sir: (Dear Admiral Hines)

Admiral/*Rear* Admiral/*Vice* Admiral Ivan I. Ives, U.S.N.
(local address)
Sir: (Dear Admiral Ives)

h. Navy Captain

Captain Jason J. Jagger, U.S.N.
(local address)
Dear Captain Jagger:

i. Navy Commodore or Commander

Commodore/Commander/Lieutenant Commander Kirk K. Kerr, U.S.N
(local address)
Dear Commodore Kerr: (Dear Commander Kerr)

j. Navy Chaplain

Chaplain Lance L. Langston, Captain, U.S.N
(local address)
Dear Chaplain Langston:

k. Navy Lieutenant or Ensign

Lieutenant/Lieutenant Junior Grade Morris M. Morrison, U.S.N.
(local address)
Dear Mr. Morrison:

Ensign Newton N Nimoy, U.S.N.
(local address)
Dear Mr. Nimoy:

l. Warrant Officer, Army or Navy

Mr. Orson O. Ott, *U.S.A./U.S.N.*
(local address)
Dear Mr. Ott:

(8) Religious Persons, Catholic

a. Abbot

The Right Reverend Adam A. Addams
Abbot of (name) Abbey
(local address)
Dear Father Abbot: (Dear Father Addams)

b. Apostolic Delegate

His Excellency, The Most Reverend Bernard B. Brooks
Archbishop of (name)
The Apostolic Delegate
Washington, D.C.
Your Excellency: (My dear Archbishop)

c. Archbishop

The Most Reverend Caesar C. Carroll
Archbishop of (place)
(local address)
Your Excellency: (Dear Archbishop Carroll)

d. Bishop

The Most Reverend Daniel D. Dolan, D.D.
Bishop of (place)

(local address)
Your Excellency: (Dear Bishop Dolan)

e. Brother

Brother Elias E. Elwood
(local address)
Dear Brother Elwood:

f. Canon

The Reverend Frances F. Fitzhugh, D.D.
Canon of (name) Cathedral
(local address)
Dear Canon Fitzhugh:

g. Cardinal

His Eminence, George Cardinal Grimes
Archbishop of (place)
(local address)
Your Eminence:

h. Member of Community

Mother Helen Hogan, R.S.C.J.
Convent of (name)
(local address)
Dear Mother Hogan:

i. Monsignor

The Right (Very) Reverend Msgr. John J. Jones
(local address)
Right Reverend and Dear Monsignor Jones:
Very Reverend and Dear Monsignor Jones:
(Dear Monsignor Jones)

j. Mother Superior

The Reverend Mother Superior, O.C.A.
College of (name)
(local address)
Dear Reverend Mother: (Dear Mother Superior)

k. The Pope

His Holiness the Pope

or
His Holiness Pope (name and number)
Vatican City
Your Holiness:

l. Priest

(*with scholastic degree*)
The Reverend Kenneth K. Kennedy, Ph.D.
(local address)
Dear Dr. Kennedy:

(*no degree*)
The Reverend Lawrence L. Lee
(local address)
Dear Father Lee:

m. Sister

Sister Maria Theresa
(local address)
Dear Sister: (Dear Sister Maria Theresa)

n. Sister Superior

The Reverend Sister Superior
Convent of (name)
(local address)
Dear Sister Superior:

o. Superior of Brotherhood

The Very Reverend Nolan N. Neal, M.M.
Director
(name of institution)
(address)
Dear Father Superior:

(9) Religious Persons, Hebrew

Rabbi

(*without degree*) Rabbi Isaac I. Ingels
(*with degree*)
Rabbi Isaac I. Ingels, Ph.D. (Dr. Isaac I. Ingels)
(local address)
Sir: (Dear Rabbi Ingels, Dear Dr. Ingels)

(10) Religious Persons, Protestant

a. Bishop, Methodist

The Reverend Otis O. Orville
Methodist Bishop
(local address)
Reverend Sir: (Dear Bishop Orville)

b. Bishop, Protestant Episcopal

The Right Reverend the Bishop of (place)
(local address)
or:
The Right Reverend Peter P. Peters, D.D., LL.D.
Bishop of (place)
(local address)
Right Reverend Sir: (Dear Bishop Peters)

c. Deacon, Archdeacon, Protestant Episcopal

The Venerable Edward E. Quinn, D.D.
The Archdeacon of (place)
(local address)
Venerable Sir: (My dear Archdeacon)

d. Dean

The Very Reverend Reginald R. Recklam, D.D.
Dean of the Cathedral of (name)
(local address)
Dear Dean Recklam:

e. Episcopal Priest

(*scholastic degree*)
The Reverend Saul S. Salk, D.D., Litt.D.
(local address)
Dear Dr. Salk:

(*no degree*)
The Reverend Terence T. Tobias
(local address)
Dear Mr. Tobias: (Dear Father Tobias)

f. Protestant Minister

(*scholastic degree*)
The Reverend Uriah U. Unger, D.D. Litt.D.
(local address)
Dear Dr. Unger:

(*no degree*)
The Reverend Valentine V. Vivian
(local address)
Dear Mr. Vivian:

(11) United Nations

a. Foreign Representative, Ambassador

His Excellency, Armond A. Aumont
Representative of (country) to the United Nations
New York, New York 10017
Excellency: (Dear Mr. Ambassador)

b. Secretary General

His Excellency, Brook B. Britt
Secretary General of the United Nations
New York, New York 10017
Excellency: (Dear Mr. Secretary General)

c. Under Secretary

The Honorable Carlton C. Carne
Under Secretary of the United Nations
The Secretariat
United Nations
New York, New York 10017
Sir: (Dear Mr. Carne)

d. United States Representative, Ambassador

The Honorable Donald D. Donnelly
United States Representative to the United Nations
New York, New York 10017
Dear Mr. Ambassador:

e. United States Representative to Council

The Honorable Edsel E. Edgar

United States Representative to the (name) Council
   of the United Nations
New York, New York 10017
Sir: (Dear Mr. Edgar)

f. United States Senior Representative to General Assembly

The Honorable Fitzgerald F. Foy
Senior Representative of the United States to
   the General Assembly of the United Nations
New York, New York 10017
Sir: (Dear Mr. Foy)

(12) Women, Divorced, Married, Widowed

a. Divorcee

Mrs. Allison Ames (her maiden name combined with former
   husband's surname)

or

Mrs. Alice Ames
(local address)
Dear Mrs. Ames:

b. Married Woman, Businesswoman

Mrs. Betty Brown
(local address)
Dear Mrs. Brown:

c. Married Woman, Otherwise

Mrs. Bruce Brown
(local address)
Dear Mrs. Brown:

d. Widow, Businesswoman

Mrs. Catherine Caldwell
(local address)
Dear Mrs. Caldwell:

e. Widow, Otherwise

Mrs. Charles Caldwell
(local address)
Dear Mrs. Caldwell:

(13) Closings

a. Formal

Very truly yours,
Respectfully yours, (Foreign Official, Governor,
    U.S. Government Executives, Religious Figures)
Very respectfully yours, (The President)

b. Informal

Sincerely yours,
Very sincerely yours,
Cordially,
Sincerely,

(14) References

a. Court Officials

Associate Justice U.S.	Mr. Justice Ace
Retired Justice U.S.	Mr. Justice Bing
Chief Justice State	Mr. Chief Justice Crane
	or Judge Crane
Chief Justice U.S.	The Chief Justice
Judge	Judge Dent
Presiding Justice	Mr. Justice, *or* Judge Edge

b. Educational Officials

Chaplain	Chaplain Ade *or* Dr. Ade
Dean	Dean Bond
	or Dr. Bond, the Dean of (school)
Doctor's Degree	Dr. Caine
Instructors, Principals	Dr. (*or* Mr.) Dark
Professors	Professor Elkins

c. Foreign Officials

Ambassadors	The Ambassador of (country)
	or: The Ambassador
	Mr. Ackerman
	(Title) Brandywine
Charge d'Affaires	Mr. Champs
Ministers	The Minister of (country)
	or: The Minister

	Mr. Danton
Premiers	Mr. Eglise
	or: The Premier
Presidents	President Foche
	or: The President
Prime Ministers	Mr. Griere
	or: The Prime Minister

d. Government Official, State and Local

Governor	Governor Able, The Governor, (outside his state) The Governor of (state)
Lieutenant Governor	Mr. Brace, The Lieutenant Governor, (outside his state) The Lieutenant Governor of (state)
Mayor	Mayor Chase
State Representative	Representative Domes Mr. Domes
State Senator	Senator Esty

e. Government Official, U.S. Cabinet

Secretaries	The Secretary of (Department), Mr. Forte The Secretary Mr. Forte *(or* Miss or Mrs. Forte)
Postmaster General	The Postmaster General, Mr. Grimes The Postmaster General Mr. Grimes
Attorney General	The Attorney General, Mr. Holmes The Attorney General Mr. Holmes

f. Government Official, Congress

Representative	Mr. Islip, Congressman from (state) Mr. Islip Mrs. (Miss) Jason, Representative from (state) Mrs. (Miss) Jason
Senator-elect	Senator-elect Koestler
Senator (or former)	Senator Lane
Speaker of House	The Speaker Mr. Meehan The Speaker, Mr. Meehan

Senate Committee Chairman	The Chairman Senator Nixon

g. Government Official, Executive

The President	The President
Former President	Former President Otis Mr. Otis
Vice President	The Vice President

h. Military Personnel

Chaplain	Captain, Chaplain, or Father Palmer
Officer	(Title) Quisling
Warrant Officer	Mr. Rieser

i. Religious Persons

Pope	His Holiness The Pope
Apostolic Delegate	The Apostolic Delegate
Archbishop, Bishop, Canon, Brother, Monsignor	(Title) (Name)
Cardinal	His Eminence Cardinal Soames
Superior of Brotherhood	Father Thames
Priest (degree) (other)	Dr. Underwood Father Villiers
Sister Superior	The Sister Superior Sister Mary Martha
Mother Superior	Reverend Mother Mother Weeks
Rabbi	Rabbi Ziegler Dr. Ziegler (degree)
Archdeacon, Dean	(Title) (Name)
Episcopal Priest	Father Andrews Mr. Andrews Dr. Andrews (degree)
Protestant Minister	Dr. Brandon Mr. Brandon

j. United Nations

Foreign Representative (Ambassador)	Mr. Ambassador The Representative of (country) to the United Nations The Ambassador Mr. Alexander
Secretary General	The Secretary General of the United Nations
U.S. Representative (Ambassador)	Mr. Ambassador Madam Ambassador The United States Representative to the United Nations Mr. Bangor *Mrs./Miss* Bangor